P9-CJH-189

Better Homes and Gardens.
CHOCOLATE

© Copyright 1984 by Meredith Corporation, Des Moines, Iowa.
All Rights Reserved. Printed in the United States of America.
First Edition. Second Printing, 1984.
Library of Congress Catalog Card Number: 83-61321
ISBN: 0-696-01305-3

ON THE COVER:
Feathery Fudge Cake (see recipe, page 10)
Chocolate Sour Cream Frosting (see recipe, page 19)
Chocolate Curls (see instructions, page 90)

BETTER HOMES AND GARDENS® BOOKS
Editor: Gerald M. Knox
Art Director: Ernest Shelton
Managing Editor: David A. Kirchner

Food and Nutrition Editor: Nancy Byal
Department Head, Cook Books: Sharyl Heiken
Associate Department Heads: Sandra Granseth, Rosemary C. Hutchinson,
    Elizabeth Woolever
Senior Food Editors: Julie Henderson, Julia Malloy, Marcia Stanley
Associate Food Editors: Jill Burmeister, Molly Culbertson, Linda Foley,
    Linda Henry, Joyce Trollope, Diane Yanney
Recipe Development Editor: Marion Viall
Test Kitchen Director: Sharon Stilwell
Test Kitchen Home Economists: Jean Brekke, Kay Cargill, Marilyn Cornelius,
    Maryellyn Krantz, Dianna Nolin, Marge Steenson

Associate Art Directors: Linda Ford Vermie, Neoma Alt West, Randall Yontz
Copy and Production Editors: Marsha Jahns, Mary Helen Schiltz,
    Carl Voss, David A. Walsh
Assistant Art Directors: Harijs Priekulis, Tom Wegner
Senior Graphic Designers: Alisann Dixon, Lynda Haupert, Lyne Neymeyer
Graphic Designers: Mike Burns, Mike Eagleton, Deb Miner, Stan Sams,
    D. Greg Thompson, Darla Whipple, Paul Zimmerman

Vice President, Editorial Director: Doris Eby
Group Editorial Services Director: Duane L. Gregg

General Manager: Fred Stines
Director of Publishing: Robert B. Nelson
Vice President, Retail Marketing: Jamie Martin
Vice President, Direct Marketing: Arthur Heydendael

CHOCOLATE
Editor: Linda Foley
Copy and Production Editor: Marsha Jahns
Graphic Designer: Stan Sams
Electronic Text Processor: Renae Piper

Our seal assures you that every recipe in *Chocolate* has
been tested in the Better Homes and Gardens® Test
Kitchen. This means that each recipe is practical and
reliable, and meets our high standards of taste appeal.

Contents

CHOCOLATE

All About Chocolate

Ahhhhh . . .chocolate. The mere thought of this word can bring a smile to the faces of young and old alike. Chocolate is truly an all-time favorite food.

Chocolate comes from pods of the cacao tree, which grows only in hot, rainy climates. When ripe, the cacao beans are removed from the pods and are put through a series of processing steps before they are transformed into the various forms of chocolate.

Throughout this book you'll discover recipes that use every type of chocolate, so you're sure to find several that especially suit your taste. To start, read the information on melting, storing, and substituting chocolate to make certain of complete success every time you cook with chocolate. The information on identifying chocolate and cocoa products, on pages 6 and 7, will help you to become familiar with the different chocolate products that are available.

Next, browse through the many luscious recipes that make the most of chocolate. You'll find everything from sinfully rich cakes and pies to elegant tortes and mousses. You'll also find valuable information about dipping your own chocolates in the Cookies and Candies chapter. And, in other chapters you'll find recipes for making homemade chocolate croissants and

crème de cacao. The grand finale of the book is a special section on garnishing with chocolate—those special touches that add an impressive finish to anything chocolate. For those times when you're too rushed to spend a lot of time in the kitchen, we've included a delightful selection of "short & sweet" recipes. These recipes take little time to prepare, yet don't skimp on quality. Look for the label "short & sweet" near the title of the recipes. You'll find all types of short-and-sweet recipes throughout the book.

Melting Chocolate

You can use any of several methods to melt chocolate, depending on the equipment you have available and the type of recipe. But, whichever method you choose, follow these general rules to assure delicious results.

First, make sure all the equipment you use for melting the chocolate is completely dry. Any moisture in the melting container or on the utensils may cause the chocolate to stiffen. If this happens, stir shortening or cooking oil into the melted chocolate, using ½ to 1 teaspoon shortening or oil for every ounce of melted chocolate. Do not substitute butter or margarine because they contain a small amount of water.

Second, never try to rush the melting process by increasing the heat.

Chocolate scorches easily and should not be used once this happens. Before melting, coarsely chop the chocolate for quicker, more even melting, if desired. You will get best results by melting chocolate slowly and evenly, stirring as directed.

Third, keep in mind that various chocolates have different consistencies when they melt. Unsweetened chocolate tends to liquefy when it melts. Semisweet, sweet, and milk chocolate hold their shape when they melt and should be stirred till smooth. In general, unsweetened chocolate is the thinnest when melted and milk chocolate is the thickest.

Listed below are several methods for melting chocolate. Choose the method that is right for each situation.

Direct Heat: This is a common and convenient method for melting chocolate. Place the chocolate in a heavy saucepan over low heat, stirring constantly till the chocolate begins to melt. Immediately remove the chocolate from the heat and stir till smooth.

Double Boiler: This is one of the best methods to use to avoid scorching the chocolate. Place water in the bottom of a double boiler so that it comes to within ½ inch of the upper pan (water should not touch the upper pan). Put the chocolate in the upper pan of the double boiler and place it over the water in the lower pan. Place the double boiler over low heat. Stir constantly till chocolate is melted. (The water in the double boiler should not come to boiling while the chocolate is melting.)

Water Bath: This method works well when melting a small amount of chocolate. Place the chocolate in a custard cup or small bowl; carefully set the cup in a pan of hot (not boiling) water over *very low* heat. Stir constantly till chocolate is just melted, making sure that none of the water splashes into the chocolate. Remove the cup from the water and stir till the chocolate is smooth.

Microwave Oven: The counter-top microwave oven is handy for melting chocolate quickly and safely. To melt chocolate pieces, place chocolate in a glass measure or a custard cup. Micro-cook chocolate pieces, uncovered, on high power till chocolate is almost melted. Remove from oven and stir till melted and smooth. Allow 1 to 1½ minutes for ½ of a 6-ounce package (½ cup) or 1½ to 2 minutes for one 6-ounce package (1 cup) chocolate pieces. To melt chocolate squares, unwrap the chocolate and place it in a custard cup or small nonmetal bowl. Micro-cook, uncovered, on high power till chocolate is almost melted. Remove from oven and stir till melted and smooth. Allow 1½ to 1¾ minutes for one square (1 ounce) or 1¾ to 2 minutes for two squares (2 ounces) chocolate. Note: Stirring is important when melting any chocolate in the microwave oven because the melted chocolate will frequently hold its shape and will not flow. Stirring helps to determine whether the chocolate is melted, and therefore allows you to stop micro-cooking before the chocolate scorches.

Oven: If you've had your oven on for another use, you can take advantage of the lingering heat to melt chocolate. Place the chocolate in a small oven-proof bowl; set the bowl in the *warm* oven. When the chocolate is almost melted, remove the bowl and stir the chocolate till it is melted and smooth.

Storing Chocolate

How you store your chocolate can affect its quality. It is important to keep chocolate in a cool, dry place. Optimum storage conditions are between 60° and 78°, with less than 50 percent relative humidity. You also can refrigerate chocolate, but tightly wrap it so it doesn't absorb odors from other foods and so moisture doesn't condense on the chocolate when it is removed from the refrigerator. Chocolate becomes hard and brittle when cold, so let it stand, tightly wrapped, at room temperature before using.

When stored at temperatures warmer than 78°, the cocoa butter in the chocolate will melt and rise to the surface, creating a gray film called "bloom." This film affects the appearance, but not the quality or flavor, of the chocolate. The chocolate will regain its original color when it is used in baking or cooking.

Cocoa powder is less sensitive to storage conditions than chocolate. But, it's still a good idea to store cocoa powder in a tightly covered container in a cool, dry place. Cocoa powder tends to lump and lose some of its rich brown color when stored at high temperatures or high humidity.

Chocolate Substitutions

When cooking with chocolate, it's best to use the type of chocolate specified in the recipe. If you find that you have a different type than what is called for, you needn't change your plans. Below are guidelines for you to use when the need for substituting chocolate arises.

● *One square (1 ounce) unsweetened chocolate,* melted: Substitute one 1-ounce envelope pre-melted unsweetened chocolate product *or* 3 tablespoons unsweetened cocoa powder plus 1 tablespoon shortening or cooking oil.

● *Unsweetened cocoa powder:* Substitute equal amounts of Dutch process cocoa powder.

● *Semisweet chocolate squares:* Substitute semisweet chocolate pieces as follows:
one square (1 ounce)=
  3 tablespoons pieces,
two squares (2 ounces)=
  ⅓ cup pieces,
three squares (3 ounces)=
  ½ cup pieces,
four squares (4 ounces)=
  ⅔ cup pieces, and
six squares (6 ounces)=
  1 cup pieces.

● *One square (1 ounce) semisweet chocolate:* Substitute one square (1 ounce) unsweetened chocolate plus 1 tablespoon sugar.

● *6 ounces semisweet chocolate:* Substitute 6 tablespoons unsweetened cocoa powder plus ¼ cup sugar and ¼ cup shortening.

● *4 ounces German sweet cooking chocolate:* Substitute ¼ cup unsweetened cocoa powder plus ⅓ cup sugar and 3 tablespoons shortening.

Identifying Chocolate and Cocoa Products

Unsweetened cocoa powder is pure chocolate with most of the cocoa butter removed. After the cocoa butter is extracted from the pure chocolate, the remaining chocolate solids are ground into unsweetened cocoa powder. (*Dutch process cocoa powder* is unsweetened cocoa powder treated with alkali, which makes it darker and slightly less bitter.) Unsweetened cocoa powder is available in 8- or 16-ounce cans and is primarily used for cooking, baking,

and making beverages. *Unsweetened chocolate* is pure chocolate with no sugar or flavorings added. It's made from cocoa beans that undergo processing. The resulting mixture is then molded into squares. Also called bitter or baking chocolate, it is available in 8-ounce packages of 1-ounce squares. *German sweet cooking chocolate* is a chocolate product made of pure chocolate, extra cocoa butter, and sugar. This type of

chocolate must contain at least 15 percent pure chocolate. It is sold in 4-ounce bars and is primarily used in baking and cooking. *Semisweet chocolate* is a chocolate product made of pure chocolate, extra cocoa butter, and sugar (less sugar than in German chocolate). This type of chocolate must contain at least 35 percent pure chocolate. It is sold in the form of chocolate pieces (6- and 12-ounce packages) and in 8-ounce packages of 1-ounce squares.

1—**Unsweetened cocoa powder**
2—**Unsweetened chocolate**
3—**German sweet cooking chocolate**
4—**Semisweet chocolate**
5—**Milk chocolate**
6—**Confectioner's coating**
7—**Pre-melted unsweetened chocolate product**
8—**Presweetened cocoa powder**
9—**Chocolate-flavored syrup**
10—**Instant cocoa mix**
11—**Fudge topping**

Milk chocolate is a chocolate product made of pure chocolate, extra cocoa butter, sugar, and milk solids. It contains at least 10 percent pure chocolate and 12 percent whole milk solids. It is the most popular eating chocolate and is sold in various-size bars and shapes.

Confectioner's coating is a general term used for a variety of chocolate-like products that have most of the cocoa butter removed and replaced by another vegetable fat. It is flavored with vanilla, vanillin, or other flavors, and is frequently tinted with vegetable coloring. It contains no chocolate flavor and may not have the same melting properties as real chocolate. Sometimes called white chocolate, almond bark, or summer coating, it is available in 2-pound packages and in blocks or round disks where candy-making supplies are sold.

Pre-melted unsweetened chocolate product is a semi-liquid chocolate-flavored product made of cocoa powder and vegetable oil. It is available in 8-ounce packages of 1-ounce envelopes and is primarily used for baking.

Presweetened cocoa powder is a powdered drink mix made of cocoa powder, sugar, and other flavorings, used to make cold and hot beverages by adding milk. It is available in 8-, 16-, and 32-ounce cans.

Chocolate-flavored syrup is a syrup product made of pure chocolate or cocoa powder, corn syrup, water, and other flavorings. It is available in jars and cans and is used as a sauce, in baking, and in making beverages.

Instant cocoa mix is a powdered drink mix made of sugar, cocoa powder, milk solids, and other flavorings. Used to make hot beverages by adding hot water, instant cocoa mix is available in 1-ounce envelopes and in various container sizes.

Fudge topping is a chocolate-flavored product similar to chocolate-flavored syrup, but thicker. It is made of pure chocolate or cocoa powder, sugar, milk, cream or butter, and is frequently used as a topping for ice cream and desserts. It is available in various container sizes.

9

10

6

11

7

8

CHOCOLATE

Cakes

Chocolate Strawberry Shortcake

The chocolate-coated strawberries make this dessert even more delicious—

6   cups fresh strawberries
¼   cup sugar
1   square (1 ounce) semisweet chocolate
1⅔   cups all-purpose flour
⅓   cup unsweetened cocoa powder
¼   cup sugar
1   tablespoon baking powder
¼   teaspoon salt
½   cup butter *or* margarine
1   beaten egg
⅔   cup milk
1   cup whipping cream
2   tablespoons sugar

Select 4 strawberries; set aside. Slice the remaining berries. Combine sliced berries and ¼ cup sugar; set aside. Melt semisweet chocolate (see instructions on page 4). Line a baking sheet with waxed paper. Spoon melted chocolate over the bottom half of each reserved strawberry. Place on baking sheet; refrigerate till needed.

For shortcake, in a mixing bowl combine flour, cocoa powder, ¼ cup sugar, baking powder, and salt. Cut in the butter or margarine till mixture resembles coarse crumbs. Combine egg and milk; add all at once to dry ingredients and stir just to moisten. Spread dough in a greased 8x1½-inch round baking pan, building up edge slightly. Bake in a 450° oven for 15 to 18 minutes or till done.

Cool 10 minutes on a wire rack. Remove from pan; place on a serving plate. Beat whipping cream and the 2 tablespoons sugar on medium speed of electric mixer till soft peaks form. Arrange some sliced berries atop cake. Spoon whipped cream over top. Arrange chocolate-coated strawberries atop whipped cream. Serve shortcake warm. Pass remaining sliced berries. Makes 8 servings.

Chocolate Sheet Cake

2   cups all-purpose flour
2   cups sugar
1   teaspoon baking soda
½   teaspoon salt
1   cup butter *or* margarine
1   cup water
⅓   cup unsweetened cocoa powder
2   eggs
½   cup buttermilk
1½   teaspoons vanilla
¼   cup butter *or* margarine
3   tablespoons unsweetened cocoa powder
3   tablespoons buttermilk
2¼   cups sifted powdered sugar
½   teaspoon vanilla
¾   cup coarsely chopped pecans

Grease and lightly flour a 15x10x1-inch or a 13x9x2-inch baking pan; set aside. In a large mixer bowl stir together flour, sugar, baking soda, and salt. In a medium saucepan combine the 1 cup butter or margarine, water, and the ⅓ cup unsweetened cocoa powder. Bring the mixture just to boiling, stirring constantly. Remove from heat. Add the mixture to the dry ingredients, beating on low speed of electric mixer just till combined. Add eggs, the ½ cup buttermilk, and the 1½ teaspoons vanilla; beat on low speed for 1 minute (batter will be thin). Turn batter into prepared pan. Bake in a 350° oven about 25 minutes for the 15x10x1-inch cake, or for 30 to 35 minutes for the 13x9x2-inch cake, or till the cake tests done.

Meanwhile, in medium saucepan combine the ¼ cup butter or margarine, 3 tablespoons unsweetened cocoa powder, and 3 tablespoons buttermilk; bring to boiling. Remove from heat. Add powdered sugar and ½ teaspoon vanilla; beat till smooth. Stir in pecans. Pour hot frosting mixture over the warm cake, spreading evenly. Cool cake on a wire rack. Makes 12 to 15 servings.

Chocolate-Cinnamon Sheet Cake: Prepare Chocolate Sheet Cake as above, *except* stir 1 teaspoon ground *cinnamon* into the dry ingredients.

Pictured opposite: Chocolate Strawberry Shortcake

Feathery Fudge Cake

This luscious chocolate creation is pictured on the cover—

3 squares (3 ounces) unsweetened chocolate
2 cups all-purpose flour
1¼ teaspoons baking soda
½ teaspoon salt
⅔ cup butter *or* margarine
1¾ cups sugar
1 teaspoon vanilla
2 eggs
1¼ cups cold water
1 square (1 ounce) semisweet chocolate
4 fresh strawberries
Whipped Chocolate Filling (optional)
Chocolate Sour Cream Frosting (see recipe, page 19)
Chocolate Curls (see instructions, page 90)

Grease and lightly flour two 9x1½-inch round baking pans; set aside. Melt the unsweetened chocolate (see instructions on page 4); cool. Stir together the flour, baking soda, and salt. In a large mixer bowl beat butter or margarine on medium speed of electric mixer about 30 seconds. Add sugar and vanilla and beat till well combined. Add eggs, one at a time, beating well on medium speed. Stir in the melted and cooled unsweetened chocolate. Add dry ingredients and cold water alternately to beaten mixture, beating on low speed after each addition. Turn batter into prepared pans. Bake in a 350° oven for 30 to 35 minutes or till cake tests done. Place on wire racks; cool 10 minutes. Remove from pans; cool thoroughly on racks.

Melt the semisweet chocolate. Line a baking sheet with waxed paper. Spoon melted chocolate over the bottom half of each strawberry. Place on baking sheet; refrigerate till needed. If using the Whipped Chocolate Filling, halve cake layers horizontally, making 4 layers. Spread the filling between the cake layers. Frost top and sides with Chocolate Sour Cream Frosting. Garnish with chocolate-coated strawberries and Chocolate Curls. Makes 12 servings.

Whipped Chocolate Filling: In a 1-cup glass measure soften ½ teaspoon *unflavored gelatin* in 1 tablespoon cold *water*. Place cup in a saucepan containing about 1 inch water; stir over low heat till dissolved. Remove saucepan from heat. In a small mixer bowl beat together 1 cup *whipping cream*, 3 tablespoons *sugar*, and 2 tablespoons *unsweetened cocoa powder* till slightly thickened. Add the dissolved gelatin all at once; beat till soft peaks form.

Devil's Food Cake

This all-time favorite cake is known for its characteristic red tint—

2¼ cups all-purpose flour
½ cup unsweetened cocoa powder
1½ teaspoons baking soda
1 teaspoon salt
½ cup shortening
1 cup sugar
1 teaspoon vanilla
3 egg yolks
1⅓ cups cold water
3 egg whites
¾ cup sugar

Grease and lightly flour two 9x1½-inch round baking pans; set aside. Stir together the flour, cocoa powder, baking soda, and salt. In a large mixer bowl beat the shortening on medium speed of electric mixer about 30 seconds. Add the 1 cup sugar and vanilla and beat till fluffy. Add the egg yolks, one at a time, beating well on medium speed.

Add the dry ingredients and cold water alternately to beaten mixture, beating on low speed after each addition just till combined. Wash the beaters thoroughly. In a small mixer bowl beat the egg whites on medium speed of electric mixer till soft peaks form (tips curl over); gradually add the ¾ cup sugar, beating till stiff peaks form (tips stand straight). Fold into cake batter. Turn into prepared pans. Bake in a 350° oven for 30 to 35 minutes or till the cake tests done. Place the cake layers on wire racks; cool for 10 minutes. Remove from pans; cool. Frost as desired. Makes 12 servings.

Black Forest Cake

Cherry Filling
⅔ cup sugar
½ cup milk
3 squares (3 ounces) unsweetened chocolate, coarsely chopped
1 slightly beaten egg
1¾ cups all-purpose flour
1 teaspoon baking soda
½ teaspoon salt
½ cup shortening
1 cup sugar
1 teaspoon vanilla
2 eggs
1 cup milk
Golden Butter Frosting
Maraschino cherries
Chocolate Curls (see instructions, page 90)

Prepare Cherry Filling. Grease and lightly flour two 9x1½-inch round baking pans; set aside. In a saucepan combine ⅔ cup sugar, the ½ cup milk, chocolate, and 1 egg. Cook and stir just till mixture boils; cool. Meanwhile, stir together flour, baking soda, and salt. In a large mixer bowl beat shortening on medium speed of electric mixer about 30 seconds. Add the 1 cup sugar and vanilla; beat till fluffy. Add the 2 eggs, one at a time, beating well on medium speed. Add dry ingredients and the 1 cup milk alternately to beaten mixture, beating after each addition. Stir in chocolate mixture. Turn into prepared pans. Bake in a 350° oven for 25 to 30 minutes or till a wooden pick inserted in the center comes out clean. Cool 10 minutes on wire racks. Remove from pans; cool thoroughly.

To assemble, place 1 cake layer on a serving plate. Use *½ cup* of the Golden Butter Frosting to make a solid circle, about 2½ inches in diameter and 1 inch high, in center of bottom cake layer. Use *1 cup* frosting to make a border, ½ inch wide and 1 inch high, around the edge of the layer. Spoon chilled Cherry Filling between circle and border. Place second cake layer on top. Frost top and sides with remaining frosting. Garnish with maraschino cherries and Chocolate Curls. Chill. Let stand at room temperature 10 minutes before serving. Makes 12 servings.

Cherry Filling: Drain one 16-ounce can pitted *dark sweet cherries,* reserving ½ cup syrup. Coarsely chop cherries and place in a bowl. Add ⅓ cup *Kirsch or cherry liqueur;* let stand 2 hours. In a saucepan combine 4 teaspoons *cornstarch* and the reserved ½ cup cherry syrup; stir in chopped cherry mixture. Cook and stir till thickened and bubbly. Cook and stir 2 minutes more. Cover surface with clear plastic wrap; chill.

Golden Butter Frosting: Beat 1 cup *butter or margarine* till fluffy. Beat in 2¼ cups sifted *powdered sugar* till smooth. Add 3 *egg yolks,* beating till mixture is fluffy. Add 2¼ cups additional sifted *powdered sugar;* beat till smooth.

How To Assemble Black Forest Cake

Use ½ cup frosting to make a solid circle, about 2½ inches in diameter and 1 inch high, in the center of the bottom cake layer. Use 1 cup frosting to make a border, ½ inch wide and 1 inch high, around the edge of the layer. Spoon Cherry Filling between frosting circle and border, as shown in the photo.

German Chocolate Cake

1 4-ounce package German
   sweet cooking chocolate,
   coarsely chopped
⅓ cup water
1⅔ cups all-purpose flour
1 teaspoon baking soda
½ teaspoon salt
½ cup butter *or* margarine
1 cup sugar
1 teaspoon vanilla
3 egg yolks
⅔ cup buttermilk
3 stiff-beaten egg whites
   Coconut Pecan Frosting

Grease and lightly flour two 8x1½-inch round baking pans; set aside. In a small saucepan combine chocolate and water; cook and stir till chocolate melts. Cool. Stir together flour, baking soda, and salt. In a large mixer bowl beat butter or margarine on medium speed of electric mixer about 30 seconds. Add sugar and vanilla; beat till fluffy. Add egg yolks, one at a time, beating well on medium speed. Beat in chocolate mixture.

Add the dry ingredients and buttermilk alternately to beaten mixture, beating after each addition. Fold in beaten egg whites. Turn cake batter into prepared pans. Bake in a 350° oven for 30 to 35 minutes or till cake tests done. Place the cake layers on wire racks; cool for 10 minutes. Remove from pans; cool thoroughly. Fill and frost top with Coconut Pecan Frosting. Makes 12 servings.

Coconut Pecan Frosting: In a medium saucepan beat 1 *egg* slightly. Stir in ⅔ cup *sugar,* one 5⅓-ounce can (⅔ cup) *evaporated milk,* and ¼ cup *butter or margarine.* Cook and stir over medium heat about 12 minutes or till mixture is thickened and bubbly. Stir in one 3½-ounce can (1⅓ cups) *flaked coconut* and ½ cup chopped *pecans;* cool.

Banana-Split Cake

The combination of chocolate, strawberries, and bananas can't be beat—

3 cups all-purpose flour
2 teaspoons baking powder
1 teaspoon salt
¼ teaspoon baking soda
1 cup butter *or* margarine
1½ cups sugar
1 teaspoon vanilla
4 eggs
1 medium banana, mashed
   (½ cup)
½ cup dairy sour cream
½ cup milk
½ cup instant cocoa mix
   Strawberry Sauce

Grease and lightly flour one 10-inch fluted tube pan; set aside. Stir together flour, baking powder, salt, and baking soda. In a large mixer bowl beat butter or margarine on medium speed of electric mixer about 30 seconds. Add sugar and vanilla and beat till fluffy. Add eggs, one at a time, beating well on medium speed.

In a small mixing bowl stir together mashed banana, dairy sour cream, and milk. Add dry ingredients and banana mixture alternately to beaten mixture, beating on low speed of electric mixer after each addition just till combined. Into *1 cup* of the cake batter, fold cocoa mix; stir gently just till combined. Spoon the plain batter into prepared tube pan. Spoon cocoa batter on top of the plain batter in a ring; do not spread to edges.

Bake in a 350° oven for 60 to 70 minutes or till cake tests done. Place cake on a wire rack; cool for 10 minutes. Remove from pan; cool thoroughly on rack. Serve with Strawberry Sauce. Makes 12 servings.

Strawberry Sauce: Measure 4 cups fresh *or* frozen unsweetened *strawberries*; thaw and drain the berries, if frozen. In a saucepan crush 1 cup of the berries; halve any large remaining berries and set aside. Add 1 cup *water* to the crushed berries. Cook for 2 minutes; sieve. Combine ¾ cup *sugar* and 2 tablespoons *cornstarch*; stir into sieved mixture. Cook and stir till thickened and bubbly. Cook and stir 2 minutes more. If desired, add a few drops of *red food coloring.* Stir in the remaining berries; chill.

Sour Cream Chocolate Cake

3 squares (3 ounces)
    unsweetened chocolate
1¾ cups all-purpose flour
1 teaspoon baking soda
½ teaspoon salt
½ cup shortening
1½ cups sugar
½ teaspoon vanilla
2 eggs
½ cup dairy sour cream

Melt chocolate (see instructions on page 4); cool. Grease and lightly flour two 8x1½-inch round baking pans. Stir together flour, baking soda, and salt. Beat shortening with electric mixer about 30 seconds. Add sugar and vanilla; beat till fluffy. Add eggs, one at a time, beating well on medium speed. Stir in melted chocolate and sour cream. Add dry ingredients and 1 cup *cold water* alternately to beaten mixture, beating after each addition. Turn into prepared pans. Bake in a 350° oven for 30 to 35 minutes or till done. Cool 10 minutes on wire racks. Remove from pans; cool thoroughly. Frost as desired. Makes 12 servings.

Chocolate Chiffon Cake

4 squares (4 ounces)
    unsweetened chocolate,
    coarsely chopped
½ cup water
¼ cup sugar
2 cups all-purpose flour
1½ cups sugar
1 tablespoon baking powder
1 teaspoon salt
½ cup cooking oil
7 egg yolks
¾ cup cold water
1 teaspoon vanilla
7 egg whites
½ teaspoon cream of tartar

In a small saucepan combine chocolate, water, and the ¼ cup sugar. Cook and stir over low heat till chocolate is melted and mixture is smooth; cool.

In a large mixer bowl sift together flour, 1½ cups sugar, baking powder, and salt. Make a well in center. Add oil, egg yolks, cold water, vanilla, and chocolate mixture. Beat on low speed till combined, then on high speed about 5 minutes or till smooth. Transfer to another bowl.

Thoroughly wash beaters and large mixer bowl. In large mixer bowl beat egg whites and cream of tartar till stiff peaks form. Pour batter in a thin stream over surface of egg whites, folding in lightly by hand. Turn into an *ungreased* 10-inch tube pan. Bake in a 325° oven for 65 to 70 minutes or till cake springs back when touched lightly with finger. Invert cake in pan; cool thoroughly. Loosen cake; remove from pan. Makes 12 servings.

Chocolate and Sour Cream Marble Pound Cake

½ cup butter *or* margarine
3 eggs
3 squares (3 ounces)
    semisweet chocolate
1½ cups all-purpose flour
¼ teaspoon salt
⅛ teaspoon baking soda
1¼ cups sugar
1 teaspoon vanilla
    Few drops almond extract
½ cup dairy sour cream

Bring butter or margarine and eggs to room temperature. Grease and lightly flour a 9x5x3-inch loaf pan. Melt chocolate (see instructions on page 4); cool. Stir together flour, salt, and baking soda. In a mixer bowl beat butter or margarine on medium speed of electric mixer till fluffy. Gradually add sugar, beating till light and fluffy.

Add eggs, one at a time, beating for 1 minute after each addition; scrape bowl frequently, guiding mixture toward beaters. Add vanilla and almond extract; beat well. Add dry ingredients and sour cream alternately to beaten mixture, beating after each addition just till combined.

Divide batter in half. Stir melted chocolate into half of batter. In pan alternate spoonfuls of light and dark batters; gently stir through batters to marble. Bake in a 350° oven about 1 hour or till done. Cool 10 minutes on wire rack. Remove from pan; cool thoroughly. Makes 12 servings.

Chocolate Spice Roll-Up

This elegant cake takes only 15 minutes to prepare—

2 squares (2 ounces) semisweet chocolate
3 eggs
⅓ cup water
2 tablespoons cooking oil
1 package 1-layer-size spice cake mix *or* ½ of a package 2-layer-size (2 cups) spice cake mix
  Sifted powdered sugar
1 8-ounce container frozen whipped dessert topping, thawed
½ cup canned chocolate frosting

Line a 15x10x1-inch jelly-roll pan with foil or waxed paper; grease well. Melt chocolate (see instructions on page 4); cool. In a small mixer bowl beat eggs on high speed of electric mixer about 5 minutes or till thick and lemon colored. Gradually add water and oil, beating till well combined. Add the dry cake mix; beat for 1 minute on low speed. Spread evenly into prepared pan. Bake in a 350° oven for 12 to 15 minutes or till cake tests done.

Immediately loosen the edges of cake from pan and turn out onto a towel sprinkled with sifted powdered sugar. Peel foil or waxed paper off cake. Starting with a narrow end, carefully roll the warm cake and towel together loosely. Cool, seam side down, on a wire rack.

Stir melted chocolate into dessert topping. Unroll cake; spread the chocolate mixture to within 1 inch of edges. Roll up filled cake. In a small saucepan heat the canned frosting over low heat for 1 to 2 minutes or till of pouring consistency, stirring frequently. Pour over top of cake roll, allowing frosting to drizzle down sides. Makes 10 servings.

Chocolate Cake Roll à la Mode

Store the "frosted" cake in the freezer till serving time, if desired—

½ cup all-purpose flour
¼ cup unsweetened cocoa powder
1 teaspoon baking powder
¼ teaspoon salt
4 egg yolks
½ teaspoon vanilla
⅓ cup sugar
4 egg whites
½ cup sugar
  Sifted powdered sugar
1 quart peppermint ice cream
¼ cup crushed peppermint candies
1 4-ounce container frozen whipped dessert topping, thawed
  Crushed peppermint candies

Grease and lightly flour a 15x10x1-inch jelly-roll pan; set aside. Sift together flour, cocoa powder, baking powder, and salt. In a small mixer bowl beat egg yolks and vanilla on high speed of electric mixer about 5 minutes or till thick and lemon colored. Gradually add the ⅓ cup sugar, beating till sugar dissolves. Thoroughly wash beaters.

In a large mixer bowl beat egg whites on medium speed of electric mixer till soft peaks form (tips curl over). Gradually add the ½ cup sugar, beating on high speed till stiff peaks form (tips stand straight). Fold yolk mixture into beaten egg whites. Sprinkle flour-cocoa mixture over egg mixture; fold in lightly by hand. Spread batter evenly into prepared pan. Bake in a 375° oven for 12 to 15 minutes or till a wooden pick inserted in the center comes out clean.

Immediately loosen the edges of the cake from pan and turn out onto a towel sprinkled with sifted powdered sugar. Starting with a narrow end, carefully roll the warm cake and towel together. Cool cake, seam side down, on a wire rack. Soften peppermint ice cream by stirring and pressing it against the sides of a bowl just till pliable. Unroll cake; spread the softened ice cream to within 1 inch of the edges. Roll up cake and ice cream; freeze. To serve, stir the ¼ cup crushed peppermint candies into the whipped dessert topping. Spread over top and sides of cake. Garnish cake with additional crushed peppermint candies, if desired. Makes 10 servings.

Pictured opposite: Chocolate Spice Roll-Up

Chocolate Angel Cake

1¼ cups sifted powdered sugar
1 cup all-purpose flour
⅓ cup unsweetened cocoa powder
1½ cups egg whites (11 or 12 large)
1½ teaspoons cream of tartar
1 teaspoon vanilla
¼ teaspoon salt
1 cup sugar

Sift together powdered sugar, flour, and unsweetened cocoa powder; repeat sifting twice. In a large mixer bowl beat egg whites, cream of tartar, vanilla, and salt on medium speed of electric mixer till soft peaks form (tips curl over). Gradually add sugar, about 2 tablespoons at a time, beating on high speed till stiff peaks form (tips stand straight). Sift about ¼ of the flour mixture over the beaten egg whites; fold in lightly by hand. Repeat with remaining flour mixture, ¼ at a time. Turn batter into an *ungreased* 10-inch tube pan. Bake in a 350° oven about 1 hour or till cake tests done. Invert cake in pan; cool thoroughly. Loosen cake; remove from pan. Makes 12 servings.

Fudge Pudding Cake

A creamy pudding layer forms on the bottom while the cake bakes—

1 cup all-purpose flour
½ cup sugar
2 tablespoons unsweetened cocoa powder
2 teaspoons baking powder
½ teaspoon salt
½ cup milk
2 tablespoons cooking oil
1 teaspoon vanilla
½ cup chopped walnuts
¾ cup sugar
¼ cup unsweetened cocoa powder
1½ cups boiling water
Sifted powdered sugar

In a large mixing bowl stir together flour, the ½ cup sugar, the 2 tablespoons cocoa powder, baking powder, and salt. Add milk, oil, and vanilla; stir till smooth. Stir in nuts. Turn into an ungreased 8x8x2-inch baking pan. Combine the ¾ cup sugar and the ¼ cup cocoa powder; gradually stir in boiling water. Pour liquid mixture evenly over batter in pan. Bake in a 350° oven about 30 minutes or till a wooden pick inserted in the cake center comes out clean. Serve warm or chilled in individual dessert dishes. Sprinkle with sifted powdered sugar. Makes 8 servings.

Cocoa Zucchini Cake

2½ cups all-purpose flour
½ cup unsweetened cocoa powder
2½ teaspoons baking powder
1½ teaspoons baking soda
1 teaspoon salt
1 teaspoon ground cinnamon
¾ cup butter *or* margarine
2 cups sugar
3 eggs
3 cups finely shredded unpeeled zucchini
1 cup chopped walnuts
2 teaspoons vanilla
½ cup milk
Cream Cheese Frosting

Grease and lightly flour a 10-inch tube pan. Stir together flour, cocoa powder, baking powder, baking soda, salt, and cinnamon. In a large mixer bowl beat butter on medium speed of electric mixer about 30 seconds. Add sugar and beat till fluffy. Add eggs, one at a time, beating well on medium speed. Stir in zucchini, nuts, and vanilla.

Add dry ingredients and milk alternately to beaten mixture, beating on low speed after each addition. Turn batter into prepared pan. Bake in a 350° oven about 1 hour or till cake tests done. Cool on wire rack 10 minutes. Remove cake from pan and cool thoroughly. Frost with Cream Cheese Frosting. Makes 12 servings.

Cream Cheese Frosting: In mixer bowl beat together two 3-ounce packages softened *cream cheese,* ½ cup *butter or margarine,* and 2 teaspoons *vanilla* till fluffy. Gradually add 4 cups sifted *powdered sugar,* beating till smooth.

Chocolate Broiler Cake

1 4-ounce package German sweet cooking chocolate
½ cup butter *or* margarine
½ cup sugar
1 teaspoon vanilla
7 egg yolks
⅔ cup all-purpose flour
3 tablespoons cornstarch
7 egg whites
¼ cup sugar
3 tablespoons butter *or* margarine
2 cups sifted powdered sugar
Boiling water

Grease and line the bottom of an 8x8x2-inch baking pan with waxed paper. Grease top of paper; set aside. Melt *half* of the chocolate (see instructions on page 4); cool.

Beat ½ cup butter with electric mixer 30 seconds. Add ½ cup sugar and vanilla; beat till fluffy. Add egg yolks, one at a time, beating well. Mix flour and cornstarch; stir into beaten mixture. Divide batter in half. Stir melted chocolate into *half* of the batter. Wash beaters well. Beat egg whites till soft peaks form. Gradually add ¼ cup sugar, beating till stiff peaks form. Divide egg whites equally between plain and chocolate batters; fold in egg whites (batter may appear curdled). Spread a scant ½ cup of the chocolate batter evenly in bottom of prepared pan (layer will be thin). Place pan under broiler so that batter is 5 inches from heat. Broil 1 to 2 minutes or till baked through. Spread a scant ½ cup plain batter atop baked chocolate layer. Broil as before. Repeat, spreading with alternating batters and broiling to make a total of 8 to 10 layers. Cool in pan 10 minutes. Invert onto wire rack; remove waxed paper. Cool.

Melt together remaining chocolate and 3 tablespoons butter. Stir in powdered sugar till crumbly. Add enough boiling water (about ¼ cup) to make of drizzling consistency. Cut cake into 9 or 16 squares. Drizzle with chocolate mixture. Makes 8 or 9 servings.

How To Make Chocolate Broiler Cake

Broil a layer of chocolate batter for 1 to 2 minutes or till done. Then spread plain batter atop baked chocolate layer; broil as before. Repeat, adding batter and broiling to make a total of 8 to 10 layers, but be sure each layer is baked through before adding more batter.

After you've allowed the Chocolate Broiler Cake to cool, cut it into 9 or 16 squares. To glaze the cake, pour the warm chocolate mixture over the individual cake squares, allowing the mixture to run down the sides, as shown in the photo.

Chocolate Malt Cupcakes

You'll love the convenient directions for the fudgy frosting—

2	squares (2 ounces) unsweetened chocolate *or* two 1-ounce envelopes pre-melted unsweetened chocolate product
1	3-ounce package cream cheese, softened
¼	cup butter *or* margarine, softened
¼	cup instant malted milk powder
½	teaspoon vanilla
3	cups sifted powdered sugar
3	tablespoons milk
1¼	cups all-purpose flour
½	teaspoon baking powder
½	teaspoon baking soda
¼	teaspoon salt
2	tablespoons butter *or* margarine, softened
2	eggs
½	cup milk

If using unsweetened chocolate squares, melt chocolate (see instructions on page 4); cool. In a large mixer bowl beat softened cream cheese and the ¼ cup butter or margarine on medium speed of electric mixer till fluffy; beat in instant malted milk powder and vanilla. Alternately beat in powdered sugar and the 3 tablespoons milk. Add the melted chocolate or pre-melted chocolate product; beat till smooth. Remove 1 cup of the chocolate mixture for frosting; cover and set aside.

Stir together flour, baking powder, baking soda, and salt; set aside. Add the 2 tablespoons butter or margarine to the remaining chocolate mixture in bowl. Add eggs; beat well. Alternately add dry ingredients and the ½ cup milk, beating till well combined. Line muffin pans with paper bake cups; fill ⅔ full. Bake in a 350° oven for 20 to 25 minutes or till done. Cool and frost with reserved chocolate frosting. Makes 16 to 18 cupcakes.

Chocolate Fruitcakes

The small-size fruitcakes are perfect for gift giving—

2	squares (2 ounces) unsweetened chocolate *or* two 1-ounce envelopes pre-melted unsweetened chocolate product
1½	cups all-purpose flour
½	teaspoon baking powder
½	cup butter *or* margarine
½	cup sugar
2	eggs
¼	cup orange juice
2	tablespoons light corn syrup
6	ounces whole red *or* green candied cherries (1 cup)
4	ounces chopped mixed candied fruits and peels (about ⅔ cup)
½	cup light raisins
½	cup chopped candied pineapple
½	cup chopped walnuts
	Crème de cacao *or* orange juice

Thoroughly grease two 8x4x2-inch loaf pans or six 4½x2½x1½-inch individual loaf pans. If using unsweetened chocolate squares, melt chocolate (see instructions on page 4); cool. Stir together flour and baking powder. In a large mixer bowl beat butter or margarine on medium speed of electric mixer about 30 seconds. Add sugar and beat till fluffy. Add melted chocolate or pre-melted chocolate product; beat well. Add eggs, one at a time, beating well on medium speed. Stir together orange juice and corn syrup. Add dry ingredients and orange juice mixture alternately to beaten mixture, beating on low speed after each addition. Combine the candied cherries, mixed candied fruits and peels, light raisins, candied pineapple, and chopped nuts; fold into batter. Turn batter into prepared loaf pans (for each small loaf pan, use about ¾ cup batter).

Bake in a 300° oven about 70 minutes for the large cakes or 35 to 40 minutes for the small cakes or till a wooden pick inserted in the center comes out clean. Cool thoroughly on wire racks. Remove from pans; wrap each cake in crème de cacao- or orange juice-moistened cheesecloth. Overwrap with foil or clear plastic wrap, or place in an airtight container. Store the cakes in the refrigerator at least 1 week. Remoisten the cheesecloth as needed if cakes are stored longer than 1 week. Makes 2 large or 6 small fruitcakes.

Fudge Frosting

3 cups sugar
3 tablespoons light corn syrup
2 squares (2 ounces) unsweetened chocolate, coarsely chopped
¼ teaspoon salt
1 cup milk
¼ cup butter *or* margarine
1 teaspoon vanilla

Butter sides of a heavy 3-quart saucepan. In it combine sugar, corn syrup, chocolate, and salt; stir in milk. Cook and stir over medium heat till all the sugar dissolves and the chocolate melts. (Avoid splashing sides of pan.) Continue cooking over medium heat till 234° (soft ball stage), stirring only as necessary to prevent sticking. (The mixture should boil gently over the entire surface.) Watch closely: Above 220° the temperature rises quickly.

Remove from heat; add butter. Don't stir in butter; simply place it on top of mixture and let the heat of the mixture melt it. Let mixture cool, without stirring, till thermometer registers 110°. (At this temperature, bottom of pan should feel comfortably warm.) Add vanilla. Using a spoon, beat mixture vigorously with an up-and-over motion till of spreading consistency (this should take 5 to 6 minutes). Check the consistency frequently so frosting doesn't become too stiff. Pour and spread *immediately* atop a 13x9-inch cake. Work quickly, using a small, metal spatula to spread frosting. To smooth small areas that set up too fast, dip spatula in warm water and then smooth over these areas. Frosts top of a 13x9-inch cake.

Note: Beating the mixture to the proper consistency is the critical step in making Fudge Frosting. If beaten correctly, the frosting will be smooth and satiny. If overbeaten or if not spread immediately it will soon become too stiff to spread, but can be used as fudge.

Chocolate Butter Frosting

2 squares (2 ounces) unsweetened chocolate *or* two 1-ounce envelopes pre-melted unsweetened chocolate product
6 tablespoons butter
4½ to 4¾ cups sifted powdered sugar
¼ cup milk
1½ teaspoons vanilla

If using unsweetened chocolate squares, melt chocolate (see instructions on page 4); cool. In a small mixer bowl beat butter or margarine till light and fluffy. Gradually add about *half* of the powdered sugar, beating well. Beat in milk, vanilla, and melted chocolate or pre-melted chocolate product. Gradually beat in remaining powdered sugar. Beat in additional milk, if necessary, to make frosting of spreading consistency. Frosts tops and sides of two 8- or 9-inch layers, top of one 15x10-inch cake or pan of bar cookies, about 24 cupcakes, or about 48 cookies.

Chocolate Sour Cream Frosting

This rich and creamy frosting is pictured on the cover—

1½ cups semisweet chocolate pieces
3 tablespoons butter *or* margarine
½ cup dairy sour cream
1 teaspoon vanilla
3½ cups sifted powdered sugar

Melt together chocolate and butter or margarine (see instructions on page 4). Cool about 10 minutes. Stir in sour cream and vanilla. Gradually add powdered sugar, beating by hand till frosting is smooth and of spreading consistency. Cover and chill to store. Frosts tops and sides of two 8- or 9-inch layers or about 24 cupcakes.

CHOCOLATE

Cookies & Candies

Chocolate Crinkles

These cookies crack during baking and form cookie wrinkles, or "crinkles"—

4 squares (4 ounces)
  unsweetened chocolate
  or four 1-ounce envelopes
  pre-melted unsweetened
  chocolate product
2 cups all-purpose flour
2 teaspoons baking powder
1½ cups sugar
½ cup cooking oil
2 teaspoons vanilla
3 eggs
  Sifted powdered sugar

If using chocolate squares, melt chocolate (see instructions on page 4); cool. Combine flour and baking powder. In a large mixer bowl combine sugar, oil, vanilla, and melted chocolate or pre-melted chocolate product. Beat in eggs. Add dry ingredients; beat till well combined. Cover; chill till dough can be handled easily. Using 1 tablespoon dough for each cookie, shape into balls; roll in powdered sugar.

Place on a greased cookie sheet. Bake in a 375° oven for 10 to 12 minutes or till edges are firm and slightly browned. Remove from cookie sheet. While the cookies are still warm, roll them again in sifted powdered sugar, if desired. Cool on a wire rack. Makes about 48 cookies.

Chocolate Chip Cookies

2½ cups all-purpose flour
1 teaspoon baking soda
½ cup butter *or* margarine
½ cup shortening
1 cup packed brown sugar
½ cup sugar
2 eggs
1½ teaspoons vanilla
1 12-ounce package (2 cups)
  semisweet chocolate
  pieces
1 cup chopped walnuts *or*
  pecans

Stir together flour and baking soda. In a large mixer bowl beat butter and shortening for 30 seconds. Add brown sugar and sugar; beat till fluffy. Add eggs and vanilla; beat well. Add dry ingredients; beat till well combined. Stir in chocolate and nuts. Drop dough from a teaspoon onto an ungreased cookie sheet. Bake in a 375° oven for 8 to 10 minutes or till edges of cookies are firm and slightly browned. Cool about 1 minute. Remove from cookie sheet; cool on a wire rack. Makes about 72 cookies.

Double Chocolate Chip Cookies: Prepare Chocolate Chip Cookies as above, *except* stir ½ cup unsweetened *cocoa powder* into dry ingredients, reduce all-purpose flour to *2 cups*, and increase sugar to *1 cup*.

Oatmeal-Chocolate Chip Cookies: Prepare Chocolate Chip Cookies as above, *except* reduce all-purpose flour to *1½ cups*. Stir 2 cups *quick-cooking rolled oats* into mixture at the same time the flour mixture is added.

Checking Cookies for Doneness

It's best to check drop, sliced, and similar types of cookies early to prevent overbaking. To check the cookies for doneness, slide a metal spatula under one of the cookies. If the edges are firm and slightly browner than the rest of the cookie, it is done. If the edges are still doughy, bake the cookies a little longer.

Pictured opposite: Oatmeal-Chocolate Chip Cookies
Chocolate Crinkles
Tri-Level Brownies (see recipe, page 26)
Coconut Creams (see recipe, page 35)
Peanut Butter Bonbons (see recipe, page 35)
Chocolate-Covered Cherries (see recipe, page 36)

No-Bake Drop Cookies

You won't need to heat up the kitchen to make these saucepan goodies—

2 cups sugar
¼ cup unsweetened cocoa
    powder
½ cup milk
½ cup butter *or* margarine
1 tablespoon light corn syrup
¼ cup peanut butter
2 cups quick-cooking
    rolled oats

In a heavy saucepan stir together sugar and cocoa powder; stir in milk. Add butter or margarine and corn syrup; bring to boiling, stirring occasionally. Boil vigorously for 3 minutes. Stir in peanut butter till smooth. Stir in rolled oats till well combined.

    Return mixture to boiling. Remove from heat; beat till slightly thickened. Immediately drop mixture from a teaspoon onto waxed paper. (If mixture spreads too much, beat it a little longer.) Cool. Makes about 36 cookies.

Two-Tone Clovers

The chocolate and plain doughs bake together to form a cloverleaf—

1 square (1 ounce)
    unsweetened chocolate
    or one 1-ounce envelope
    pre-melted unsweetened
    chocolate product
1¾ cups all-purpose flour
½ teaspoon baking soda
½ teaspoon salt
½ cup butter *or* margarine
½ cup sugar
½ cup packed brown sugar
1 egg
1 teaspoon vanilla
¾ cup dairy sour cream
¼ cup chopped walnuts

If using the unsweetened chocolate square, melt chocolate (see instructions on page 4); cool. Stir together flour, baking soda, and salt. In a large mixer bowl beat butter or margarine on medium speed of electric mixer for 30 seconds. Add sugar and brown sugar and beat till fluffy. Add egg and vanilla; beat well. Stir in sour cream. Add dry ingredients to beaten mixture and beat till well combined. Stir in chopped walnuts.

    Divide dough in half. Stir the melted unsweetened chocolate or pre-melted unsweetened chocolate product into half of the dough. For each cookie, drop 2 small mounds of chocolate dough from a teaspoon side by side onto an ungreased cookie sheet. Using the plain dough, drop 2 small mounds from a teaspoon next to and touching the chocolate mounds, forming a cloverleaf. Bake in a 375° oven for 12 to 15 minutes or till plain part of cookie is golden brown. Cool about 1 minute. Remove from cookie sheet; cool on a wire rack. Makes about 24 cookies.

How To Make Two-Tone Clovers

Drop two small mounds of chocolate dough from a teaspoon side by side onto an ungreased cookie sheet. Using the plain dough, drop two small mounds from a teaspoon next to and touching the chocolate mounds, forming a cloverleaf. The mounds of dough will bake together.

Cocoa Drop Cookies

2½ cups all-purpose flour
½ cup unsweetened cocoa
  powder
1 teaspoon baking powder
1 teaspoon baking soda
½ teaspoon salt
1 cup butter or margarine
1¾ cups sugar
1 cup cream-style cottage
  cheese
2 eggs
1 teaspoon vanilla

Stir together flour, cocoa powder, baking powder, baking soda, and salt. In a large mixer bowl beat butter or margarine on medium speed of electric mixer for 30 seconds. Add sugar and cottage cheese; beat till fluffy and smooth. Add eggs and vanilla; beat well. Add dry ingredients to beaten mixture and beat till well combined.

Drop from a teaspoon 2 inches apart onto an ungreased cookie sheet. Bake in a 350° oven for 10 to 12 minutes or till edges of cookies are firm and slightly browned. Cool about 1 minute. Remove from cookie sheet; cool on a wire rack. Frost as desired. Makes about 72 cookies.

Mocha Frosted Drops

2 squares (2 ounces)
  unsweetened chocolate
  or two 1-ounce envelopes
  pre-melted unsweetened
  chocolate product
½ cup shortening
1½ cups all-purpose flour
½ teaspoon baking powder
½ teaspoon baking soda
¼ teaspoon salt
1 cup packed brown sugar
1 egg
½ cup buttermilk
1 teaspoon vanilla
1 6-ounce package (1 cup)
  semisweet chocolate
  pieces
½ cup chopped walnuts
  Mocha Butter Frosting
  Toasted coconut (optional)

If using chocolate squares, in a heavy medium saucepan melt together chocolate squares and shortening over low heat, stirring constantly. Cool 10 minutes. (If using pre-melted chocolate product, in a heavy medium saucepan melt shortening; stir in pre-melted chocolate product till well combined.) Meanwhile, stir together all-purpose flour, baking powder, baking soda, and salt. Stir brown sugar into the chocolate mixture. Add egg, buttermilk, and vanilla; beat till smooth.

Add dry ingredients to chocolate mixture and beat till well combined. Stir in chocolate pieces and nuts. Drop from a teaspoon 2 inches apart onto a greased cookie sheet. Bake in a 350° oven about 10 minutes or till edges are firm and slightly browned. Cool about 1 minute. Remove from cookie sheet; cool thoroughly on a wire rack. Frost cookies with Mocha Butter Frosting. Sprinkle with toasted coconut, if desired. Makes about 42 cookies.

Mocha Butter Frosting: In a small mixer bowl beat ¼ cup *butter or margarine,* 2 tablespoons unsweetened *cocoa powder,* and 2 teaspoons instant *coffee crystals* on medium speed of electric mixer till the mixture is fluffy. Beat in 2½ cups sifted *powdered sugar,* 1½ teaspoons *vanilla,* and enough *milk* (2 to 3 tablespoons) to make the frosting of spreading consistency.

Storing Cookies

To store cookies, place them in tightly covered containers. Store soft and crisp cookies separately or the crisp ones will become soft.

If soft cookies begin to dry out, place an apple half, skin side down, on top of the cookies in the storage container. Remove and discard the fruit after a day or two.

For ease, store bar cookies in the pan in which they were baked. Cover the baking pan tightly.

Freezing Cookies

For long-term storage, you can freeze baked cookies in freezer containers, freezer bags, or foil for up to 12 months. (It's best to pack fragile cookies in freezer containers.) Before serving, thaw the frozen cookies in the freezer wrappings. To freeze unbaked cookies, pack the dough into freezer containers or shape stiff dough into rolls; wrap securely in foil. You can store cookie dough in the freezer for up to 6 months.

Chocolate-Coconut Slices

These coconut-filled chocolate cookies are pictured on page 27—

2   squares (2 ounces)
      unsweetened chocolate
      or two 1-ounce envelopes
      pre-melted unsweetened
      chocolate product
1   3-ounce package cream
      cheese, softened
⅓   cup sugar
1   teaspoon vanilla
1   cup flaked coconut
½   cup finely chopped nuts
1½ cups all-purpose flour
½   teaspoon baking soda
½   teaspoon salt
⅓   cup butter or margarine
1   cup sifted powdered sugar
1   egg
1   teaspoon vanilla

If using unsweetened chocolate squares, melt chocolate (see instructions on page 4); cool. For the filling, in a small mixer bowl beat cream cheese, sugar, and 1 teaspoon vanilla on medium speed of electric mixer till smooth. Stir in coconut and finely chopped nuts. Cover and chill.

For the dough, in a small mixing bowl stir together flour, baking soda, and salt. In a large mixer bowl beat butter or margarine on medium speed of electric mixer for 30 seconds. Add powdered sugar, beating till well combined. Beat in egg, 1 teaspoon vanilla, and melted chocolate or pre-melted chocolate product. Add dry ingredients, beating till well combined. Cover and chill dough about 30 minutes.

Between 2 pieces of waxed paper, roll dough into a 14x4½-inch rectangle. Remove the top piece of waxed paper. Shape the coconut filling into a 14-inch-long roll; place filling on dough. Roll dough around filling, removing bottom piece of waxed paper; seal edge of dough. Wrap rolled dough and filling in waxed paper; chill several hours or overnight. Before baking, cut dough into ¼-inch slices. Place slices on a greased cookie sheet. Bake in a 375° oven for 8 to 10 minutes or till edges of cookies are firm and slightly browned. Cool about 1 minute; remove from cookie sheet. Cool on a wire rack. Makes about 48 cookies.

Chocolate Spritz

Use a cookie press to create a variety of chocolate shapes—

3   squares (3 ounces)
      semisweet chocolate
3⅔ cups all-purpose flour
1   teaspoon baking powder
1½ cups butter *or* margarine
1   cup packed brown sugar
1   egg
1   teaspoon vanilla

Melt the semisweet chocolate (see instructions on page 4); cool. In a small mixing bowl stir together flour and baking powder. In a large mixer bowl beat butter or margarine on medium speed of electric mixer for 30 seconds. Add brown sugar and beat till fluffy. Add egg, vanilla, and melted chocolate; beat well. Gradually add dry ingredients to beaten mixture, beating till well combined. *Do not chill.* Force dough through a cookie press onto an ungreased cookie sheet. Bake in a 400° oven for 6 to 7 minutes or till edges of the cookies are firm and slightly browned. Cool on a wire rack. Makes about 96 cookies.

Cocoa Cutouts

These cookies are great alone or sandwiched with your favorite frosting—

1¾ cups all-purpose flour
⅓ cup unsweetened cocoa powder
1½ teaspoons baking powder
¼ teaspoon salt
⅛ teaspoon ground cinnamon
⅓ cup shortening
⅓ cup butter *or* margarine
¾ cup sugar
1 egg
1 tablespoon milk
1 teaspoon vanilla

In a small mixing bowl stir together all-purpose flour, unsweetened cocoa powder, baking powder, salt, and cinnamon till well combined; set aside. In a large mixer bowl beat together the shortening and butter or margarine on medium speed of electric mixer for 30 seconds. Add the sugar and beat till fluffy. Add the egg, milk, and vanilla; beat well. Gradually add the dry ingredients, beating till the chocolate mixture is well combined.

Divide chocolate dough in half; cover and chill about 3 hours. Working with half of the chilled dough at a time, on a lightly floured surface roll the dough to about ⅛-inch thickness. Using cookie cutters or a knife, cut the chocolate dough into desired shapes. Place the cutout dough on an ungreased cookie sheet. Bake in a 375° oven for 6 to 8 minutes or till edges of cookies are firm and slightly browned. Cool about 1 minute. Remove the cookies from cookie sheet; cool on a wire rack. Makes 36 to 48 cookies.

Note: If desired, you can sandwich your favorite homemade or purchased frosting between two of the baked and cooled cutout cookies.

How To Make Cocoa Cutouts

Working with half of the chilled chocolate dough at a time, on a lightly floured surface roll the dough to about ⅛-inch thickness. Using cookie cutters or a knife, cut the dough into desired shapes, as shown in the photo.

After the cookies are baked and thoroughly cooled, you can sandwich two cookies together using your favorite frosting. Simply spread frosting on one of the cookies and top with another cookie, as shown in the photo.

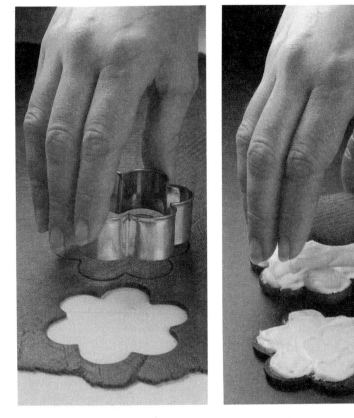

Chocolate Chip Sandies

You'll find chocolate inside and outside these tender cookies—

1 cup butter *or* margarine
⅓ cup sugar
2 teaspoons water
2 teaspoons vanilla
2 cups all-purpose flour
1 6-ounce package (1 cup) miniature semisweet chocolate pieces
½ cup chopped pecans
¼ cup sifted powdered sugar
1 tablespoon shortening

In a large mixer bowl beat butter or margarine on medium speed of electric mixer for 30 seconds. Add sugar; beat till fluffy. Add water and vanilla; beat well. Stir in flour, *half* of the chocolate pieces, and the pecans. Shape the dough into 1½x½-inch crescents. Place the crescents on an ungreased cookie sheet. Bake in a 325° oven about 25 minutes or till edges are firm and slightly browned; cool thoroughly.

In a plastic bag gently shake a few cookies at a time in powdered sugar. Melt together the remaining chocolate pieces and the shortening (see instructions on page 4). Dip one end of each cookie into the melted chocolate mixture. Place the dipped cookies on a waxed-paper-lined cookie sheet; chill till chocolate is set. Makes about 36 cookies.

Tri-Level Brownies

Enjoy three delightful layers in one bite, as pictured on page 20—

1 cup quick-cooking rolled oats
½ cup all-purpose flour
½ cup packed brown sugar
¼ teaspoon baking soda
⅓ cup butter *or* margarine, melted
1 square (1 ounce) unsweetened chocolate
¼ cup butter *or* margarine
⅔ cup all-purpose flour
⅛ teaspoon baking soda
¾ cup sugar
1 egg
½ teaspoon vanilla
¼ cup milk
½ cup chopped walnuts
1 square (1 ounce) unsweetened chocolate
2 tablespoons butter *or* margarine
1½ cups sifted powdered sugar
1 teaspoon vanilla

For bottom layer, stir together oats, the ½ cup flour, brown sugar, and the ¼ teaspoon baking soda. Stir in the ⅓ cup melted butter. Pat into an ungreased 11x7x1½-inch baking pan. Bake in a 350° oven for 10 minutes; cool.

For middle layer, melt together 1 square unsweetened chocolate and the ¼ cup butter or margarine (see instructions on page 4); cool. Stir together the ⅔ cup flour and the ⅛ teaspoon baking soda. In a mixer bowl combine sugar and the melted chocolate mixture. Add egg and the ½ teaspoon vanilla; beat just till combined. Add the flour mixture and milk alternately to chocolate mixture; stir till combined. Stir in nuts. Spread chocolate mixture over bottom layer. Bake in a 350° oven for 25 to 30 minutes or till a slight imprint remains when touched. (Do not overbake.) Cool.

For the top layer, melt together 1 square unsweetened chocolate and 2 tablespoons butter or margarine. Stir in powdered sugar and 1 teaspoon vanilla. Stir in enough *hot water* (about 2 tablespoons) to make almost pourable. Spread over brownies. Cut into bars. Makes 24.

Testing Bar Cookies for Doneness

When you bake a batch of bar cookies, use these doneness tests. For cakelike bars, such as Chocolate Cake Brownies on page 30, insert a wooden pick in the center of the bars. The wooden pick will come out clean when bars are done. For fudgelike bars, such as Tri-Level Brownies, lightly touch the surface. The bars are done when a slight imprint remains after touching.

Pictured opposite: Chocolate Nut Clusters (see recipe, page 30)
Chocolate Chip Sandies
Chocolate-Coconut Slices (see recipe, page 24)

Fudge Brownies

You can conveniently mix all the ingredients in a medium saucepan—

½ cup butter *or* margarine
2 squares (2 ounces) unsweetened chocolate
1 cup sugar
2 eggs
1 teaspoon vanilla
¾ cup all-purpose flour
½ cup chopped nuts

Grease an 8x8x2-inch baking pan; set aside. In a medium saucepan melt butter or margarine and unsweetened chocolate over low heat, stirring constantly. Remove from heat; stir in sugar. Add eggs and vanilla. Lightly beat the chocolate mixture by hand just till blended (don't overbeat because brownies will rise too high, then fall). Stir in all-purpose flour. Stir in chopped nuts. Spread the chocolate mixture in the prepared pan. Bake in a 350° oven about 30 minutes or till a slight imprint remains when touched. Cool on a wire rack. Cut into bars. Makes 16 brownies.

Chocolate Syrup Brownies

These cakelike brownies are made with chocolate-flavored syrup—

½ cup butter *or* margarine
1 cup sugar
4 eggs
1 16-ounce can (about 1½ cups) chocolate-flavored syrup
1¼ cups all-purpose flour
1 cup chopped nuts
Quick Chocolate Glaze

Grease a 13x9x2-inch baking pan; set aside. In a large mixer bowl beat butter or margarine on medium speed of electric mixer for 30 seconds. Add sugar and beat till fluffy. Add eggs; beat well. Stir in chocolate-flavored syrup. Stir in flour. (Batter will look curdled.) Fold in chopped nuts. Spread the chocolate batter in the prepared pan. Bake in a 350° oven for 30 to 35 minutes or till a wooden pick inserted in the center comes out clean. Cool slightly on a wire rack; spread with Quick Chocolate Glaze. Cut into bars. Makes 32 brownies.

Quick Chocolate Glaze: In a medium saucepan combine ⅔ cup *sugar*, 3 tablespoons *milk*, and 3 tablespoons *butter or margarine*. Heat till boiling; boil 30 seconds. Stir in ½ cup *semisweet chocolate pieces* till melted.

Chocolate Chip Bars

Now you can turn all-time favorite cookies into tasty bars—

1¼ cups all-purpose flour
½ teaspoon baking powder
⅛ teaspoon baking soda
½ cup butter *or* margarine
¾ cup packed brown sugar
1 egg
2 tablespoons milk
1 teaspoon vanilla
1 6-ounce package (1 cup) semisweet chocolate pieces

Grease a 9x9x2-inch baking pan. In a small mixing bowl stir together flour, baking powder, and baking soda. In a large mixer bowl beat butter or margarine on medium speed of electric mixer for 30 seconds. Add brown sugar and beat till fluffy. Add egg, milk, and vanilla; beat well.

Add dry ingredients to beaten mixture and beat till well combined. Stir in chocolate pieces. Spread batter in the prepared pan. Bake in a 350° oven about 30 minutes or till a wooden pick inserted in the center comes out clean. Cool on a wire rack. Cut into bars. Makes 32 brownies.

Serving Bar Cookies

It's sometimes tricky to determine how many servings you can get from a pan of bar cookies because recipes vary in yield, thickness, and richness. The number of bar cookies a recipe yields depends on the size of the pan and on the size of the serving. Bar cookies that are rich and thick, such as Chocolate Revel Bars, are cut into smaller-size servings than other bar cookies.

Although it won't alter the number of servings, you can give bar cookies a different look by cutting them into diamond shapes. To do this, make diagonal cuts in one direction and straight cuts in the other direction.

Chocolate Revel Bars

This recipe is a real favorite in our Test Kitchen—

3 cups quick-cooking rolled oats
2½ cups all-purpose flour
1 teaspoon baking soda
½ teaspoon salt
1 cup butter *or* margarine
2 cups packed brown sugar
2 eggs
2 teaspoons vanilla
1½ cups semisweet chocolate pieces
1 14-ounce can (1¼ cups) Eagle Brand sweetened condensed milk
2 tablespoons butter *or* margarine
½ cup chopped walnuts
2 teaspoons vanilla

Stir together rolled oats, flour, baking soda, and salt. In a large mixer bowl beat the 1 cup butter or margarine on medium speed of electric mixer for 30 seconds. Add brown sugar and beat till fluffy. Add eggs and 2 teaspoons vanilla; beat well. Add dry ingredients to beaten mixture and beat till well combined. In a heavy saucepan combine chocolate pieces, sweetened condensed milk, and the 2 tablespoons butter or margarine. Cook and stir over low heat till chocolate and butter or margarine are melted. Remove from heat. Stir in nuts and 2 teaspoons vanilla.

To assemble the bars, pat ⅔ of the oat mixture onto the bottom of an ungreased 15x10x1-inch baking pan. Spread the chocolate mixture atop oat mixture. Dot with the remaining oat mixture. Bake in a 350° oven for 25 to 30 minutes or till oat mixture is lightly browned (chocolate layer will still look moist). Cool on a wire rack. Cut into bars. Makes 48 bars.

How To Assemble the Chocolate Revel Bars

To assemble, pat ⅔ of the oat mixture onto the bottom of an ungreased 15x10x1-inch baking pan. Spread the chocolate mixture over the oat mixture. Dot with the remaining oat mixture, as shown in the photo.

Chocolate Cake Brownies

3 squares (3 ounces)
    unsweetened chocolate
1½ cups all-purpose flour
2 teaspoons baking powder
½ teaspoon salt
½ cup butter *or* margarine
1¼ cups sugar
2 eggs
1 teaspoon vanilla
1 cup milk
1 cup chopped walnuts
    Chocolate Frosting

Grease a 15x10x1-inch baking pan. Melt the unsweetened chocolate (see instructions on page 4); cool. Stir together the flour, baking powder, and salt. In a large mixer bowl beat the butter or margarine on medium speed of an electric mixer for 30 seconds. Add sugar and beat till the mixture is fluffy. Add eggs, vanilla, and melted unsweetened chocolate; beat well. Add the dry ingredients and milk alternately to the beaten mixture, beating after each addition. Stir in the chopped walnuts. Turn the chocolate batter into the prepared pan. Bake in a 350° oven for 18 to 20 minutes or till a wooden pick inserted in the center comes out clean. Cool on a wire rack. Frost with the Chocolate Frosting. Cut into bars. Makes 36 brownies.

Chocolate Frosting: In a heavy medium saucepan combine 2 squares (2 ounces) coarsely chopped *unsweetened chocolate*, 3 tablespoons *butter or margarine*, and ¼ cup *milk*. Cook and stir over low heat till the chocolate is melted. Stir in 3 cups sifted *powdered sugar*. Add additional *milk*, if necessary, to make the frosting of spreading consistency.

Chocolate Nut Clusters

These rich treats, pictured on page 27, take only 15 minutes to prepare—

1 6-ounce package (1 cup)
    semisweet chocolate
    pieces
6 ounces chocolate, vanilla,
    or butterscotch
    confectioner's coating,
    coarsely chopped
2 cups Spanish peanuts
    or cashews

Line a cookie sheet with waxed paper. In a heavy medium saucepan melt together the semisweet chocolate pieces and confectioner's coating over low heat, stirring constantly. Cool the mixture slightly. Stir in Spanish peanuts or cashews. For each cluster, drop a rounded teaspoonful of the mixture onto the prepared cookie sheet. Chill about 1 hour or till firm. Cover and store in the refrigerator. Makes about 24 clusters.

Rocky Road Fudge

This marshmallow-nut fudge takes only 15 to 20 minutes to mix—

2 8-ounce bars milk chocolate,
    broken into pieces
3 cups tiny marshmallows
¾ cup coarsely chopped nuts

Butter an 8x8x2-inch baking pan. In a heavy medium saucepan melt chocolate over low heat, stirring constantly. Remove from heat. Stir in the marshmallows and nuts. Spread mixture in the prepared pan. Cover and chill several hours or till firm. Cut into squares. Makes 1½ pounds of candy.

Easy Fudge

Forget the candy thermometer when preparing this 15-minute fudge—

½ cup butter *or* margarine
⅓ cup water
1 16-ounce package (4 cups) powdered sugar
½ cup nonfat dry milk powder
½ cup unsweetened cocoa powder
½ cup chopped nuts

In a saucepan heat together butter and water just to boiling, stirring to melt butter. Sift together powdered sugar, dry milk powder, and cocoa powder. (If mixture seems lumpy, sift again.) Add the butter mixture; stir till well combined. Stir in nuts. Turn into a buttered 8x8x2-inch baking pan. Cover and chill several hours or till firm. Cut into squares. Makes about 1½ pounds candy.

Old-Time Fudge

2 cups sugar
¾ cup milk
2 squares (2 ounces) unsweetened chocolate, coarsely chopped
1 teaspoon light corn syrup
2 tablespoons butter *or* margarine
½ cup coarsely chopped nuts
1 teaspoon vanilla

Butter sides of a heavy 2-quart saucepan. In it combine sugar, milk, chocolate, and corn syrup. Cook and stir over medium heat till sugar dissolves and mixture comes to boiling. Continue cooking to 234° (soft-ball stage), stirring only as necessary to prevent sticking (mixture should boil gently over surface). Immediately remove from heat; add butter but *do not stir*. Cool, without stirring, to 110° or lukewarm (should take 35 to 40 minutes). Add nuts and vanilla. Beat vigorously till fudge becomes thick and just loses its gloss (should take 7 to 10 minutes). Immediately spread in a buttered 9x5x3-inch loaf pan. Score into squares while warm; cut when firm. Makes 1¼ pounds.

Candy Testing

Using a candy thermometer is the best way to ensure success when making candy. Test the accuracy of your thermometer by placing it in boiling water. If it registers above 212°F, add the number of degrees in excess of 212°F to the recipe temperature. If it registers below 212°F, subtract the number of degrees less than 212°F from the recipe temperature.

If a thermometer is not available, use the *cold water test*. Remove the mixture from heat. Immediately drop a few drops of the syrup into a cup of very cold (but not icy) water. Use fresh water and a clean spoon for each test. Form the drops into a ball with your fingers. The firmness of the ball indicates the syrup's temperature.

Retest every 2 to 3 minutes till the desired stage is reached. The stages are: *Thread Stage* (230°F to 234°F)—candy syrup that is dropped from a spoon spins a 2-inch thread; *Soft-Ball Stage* (234°F to 240°F)—candy syrup can be shaped into a ball that flattens when removed from water; *Firm-Ball Stage* (244°F to 248°F)—candy syrup can be shaped into a firm ball that does not flatten when removed from water; *Hard-Ball Stage* (250°F to 266°F)—candy syrup forms a hard but pliable ball; *Soft-Crack Stage* (270°F to 290°F)—candy syrup separates into threads that are not hard or brittle; *Hard-Crack Stage* (300°F to 310°F)—candy syrup separates into brittle threads.

Storing Candy

The secret of making good candy is to follow the recipe directions exactly. And the secret of keeping the homemade candy at its best is to store it properly.

Individually wrap all caramels, such as the Chocolate Caramels on the opposite page, to keep out moisture, which causes the candy to stick together. Store wrapped candy in an airtight container in a cool, dry place. Protect brittles, such as the Toffee Butter Crunch, from dampness by storing them in an airtight container.

Fudge and fondant, such as the Rocky Road Fudge, Easy Fudge, and Old-Time Fudge on pages 30 and 31 and the Fondant on page 37, will stay fresh and creamy for several weeks if they are tightly wrapped in waxed paper, foil, or clear plastic wrap. Store the wrapped candy in an airtight container in a cool, dry place.

Keep chocolate-dipped candies, such as the various recipes on pages 35-37, in bonbon or candy cups and store them in a cool, dry place.

Toffee Butter Crunch

This tender, crisp toffee has a distinct buttery flavor—

1   cup butter *or* margarine
1   cup sugar
3   tablespoons water
1   tablespoon light corn syrup
½   cup coarsely chopped pecans *or* toasted almonds
¾   cup semisweet chocolate pieces
½   cup finely chopped pecans *or* toasted almonds

Butter the sides of a heavy 2-quart saucepan. In the saucepan melt the butter or margarine. Add sugar, water, and light corn syrup. Cook and stir over medium heat till sugar dissolves and mixture comes to boiling. Continue cooking to 290° (soft-crack stage), stirring only as necessary to prevent sticking (mixture should boil gently over entire surface). Watch carefully after 280°. Remove from heat. Quickly stir in the ½ cup *coarsely* chopped pecans or toasted almonds. Immediately turn the mixture onto a buttered baking sheet. Wait for 2 to 3 minutes for candy surface to firm, then sprinkle with the semisweet chocolate pieces. Let stand for 1 to 2 minutes. When the chocolate pieces are softened, spread evenly over the hardened candy; sprinkle with the ½ cup *finely* chopped pecans or toasted almonds. Chill till chocolate is firm; break into pieces. Makes about 1½ pounds.

How To Make Toffee Butter Crunch

After the surface of the candy is firm, sprinkle it with the semisweet chocolate pieces. Let stand for 1 to 2 minutes. When the chocolate pieces are softened, spread the chocolate evenly over the hardened candy, as shown in the photo.

Chocolate Nut Balls

These little goodies make a great snack—

1 6-ounce package (1 cup)
    semisweet chocolate
    pieces
2 tablespoons butter
    or margarine
1 egg
1 cup sifted powdered sugar
½ teaspoon vanilla
½ cup flaked coconut
½ cup chopped peanuts
    Flaked coconut

In a heavy medium saucepan melt together the semisweet chocolate pieces and butter or margarine over low heat, stirring frequently. Remove the saucepan from heat; cool the chocolate mixture to lukewarm.

Beat the egg into the chocolate mixture till smooth and glossy. Add the sifted powdered sugar and vanilla; mix well. Stir in the ½ cup flaked coconut and the chopped peanuts. Chill the chocolate-coconut mixture about 1 hour. Form the chilled mixture into 1-inch balls; roll the balls in additional flaked coconut. Arrange the balls on a baking sheet. Chill at least 3 hours or till the balls are firm. Makes about 30 candies.

Chocolate Turtles

These chocolate, caramel, and pecan candies are a snap to make—

1 14-ounce bag vanilla and
    chocolate caramels
⅓ cup butter *or* margarine
2 cups pecan halves
1 6-ounce package (1 cup)
    semisweet chocolate
    pieces

Remove the paper wrappers from the caramels. In a heavy medium saucepan combine the caramels and butter or margarine. Cook and stir over medium-low heat till the caramels are melted and the mixture is well combined.

To assemble each turtle candy, arrange 4 pecan halves on a greased or waxed-paper-lined baking sheet so their ends touch in a spoke fashion. Drop the caramel mixture from a teaspoon onto the center of each group of pecan halves where the 4 ends meet. Cool the clusters till the caramel is set.

Melt the semisweet chocolate pieces (see instructions on page 4). Spread the melted chocolate over the mound of caramel in each cluster. Chill the turtle candies till the chocolate is firm. Let stand at room temperature for at least 15 minutes before serving. Makes 36 candies.

Chocolate Caramels

You can dip these creamy caramels in chocolate for a double treat—

1 cup butter *or* margarine
1 16-ounce package (2½ cups
    packed) brown sugar
1 cup light corn syrup
1 14-ounce can (1¼ cups)
    Eagle Brand sweetened
    condensed milk
2 squares (2 ounces)
    unsweetened chocolate,
    coarsely chopped
1 teaspoon vanilla

Generously butter a 9x9x2-inch baking pan; set aside. In a heavy 3-quart saucepan melt the 1 cup butter or margarine. Add brown sugar; stir thoroughly. Stir in corn syrup. Gradually add sweetened condensed milk, stirring constantly. Stir in the unsweetened chocolate. Cook and stir over medium heat till the sugar dissolves and the mixture comes to boiling. Continue cooking to 245° (firm-ball stage), stirring only as necessary to prevent sticking (mixture should boil gently over entire surface). Cooking to 245° should take 15 to 20 minutes. Remove mixture from heat; stir in vanilla. Pour into the buttered pan. When cool, cut with a wet, sharp knife into ½-inch squares. Wrap each square in clear plastic wrap. Makes about 2½ pounds.

Dipping Chocolates

You can dip a variety of treats, such as caramels, nuts, pretzels, fresh or candied fruits, or homemade candy centers (see recipes, pages 35-37) into melted chocolate for luscious homemade candies.

For best results, dip chocolates on a cool, dry day (60° to 65°). Use at least 1 to 1½ pounds of semisweet chocolate, milk chocolate, or confectioner's coating for dipping. This amount ensures maximum coverage of the centers. More than 2 pounds of chocolate is difficult to keep evenly melted during the dipping process.

Finely chop chocolate or confectioner's coating so it will melt quickly and evenly. Place water in the bottom of a double boiler to within ½ inch of the upper pan; bring the water to boiling. Remove from heat. Place about *one-fourth* of the chocolate in top of double boiler; set over the hot water till chocolate begins to melt (do not return to heat). Add remaining chocolate, about ½ cup at a time, *stirring constantly* after each addition till melted and smooth. Stir till the chocolate reaches 120°. If necessary, return to heat to reach 120°.

Refill bottom of double boiler with *cool* water to within ½ inch of upper pan. Place chocolate over cool water. Stir frequently for 45 to 50 minutes or till chocolate cools to 83° (96° for confectioner's coating). Heating to 130°, then cooling to 83°, helps prevent dullness or streaking.

Follow directions below for dipping centers. Work quickly, stirring chocolate frequently to keep it evenly heated. Chocolate will stay at dipping temperature (80° to 83°; 92° to 96° for confectioner's coating) about 30 minutes. If chocolate cools to below dipping temperature, replace cool water with *lukewarm* water.

Let dipped candies stand, uncovered, till set. If dipped chocolates speckle or develop gray streaks, improper water temperature or drafts may be the causes. However, speckles or streaks affect only the appearance, not the quality or flavor, of the chocolates. (Better quality chocolate is less likely to speckle.) Cover and store the dipped candy in a cool, dry place.

How To Dip Chocolates

Drop desired centers, one at a time, into the melted chocolate or confectioner's coating; turn with a long-tined fork to coat. Lift the candy out with the fork without piercing the center. Let excess chocolate or coating drip off the fork, as shown in the photo.

Draw the bottom of the fork across the rim of the pan to remove any remaining excess chocolate or coating. Invert the dipped candy onto a waxed-paper-lined baking sheet. Twist the fork slightly as the candy falls so you can swirl the top, as shown in the photo. (If a large amount of chocolate pools at the base, next time allow more chocolate to drip off fork before inverting the candy.)

Molding Chocolates

It becomes tricky to completely coat the candy centers when you have only ½ to 1 cup of melted chocolate remaining. With this small amount, it's also hard to control the temperature of the melted chocolate. Therefore, this is a good time to stop dipping and start molding chocolates.

To make molded chocolates, stir ½ teaspoon *shortening* into each ½ to 1 cup melted chocolate. Spoon the chocolate mixture into clean, dry, plastic candy molds. If necessary, use a spatula to spread chocolate evenly in the molds. Tap the molds gently against a counter top to remove any air bubbles. You may need to use a wooden pick to remove air bubbles on the surface of the chocolate. Wipe off any excess chocolate on the mold, leaving the chocolate flush with the edge of the design. Chill for 10 to 20 minutes or till firm. To unmold, turn upside down and tap gently till chocolates release. Chill till ready to serve.

If you prefer not to make molded chocolates from leftover melted chocolate, you can make candy clusters instead. Just stir your favorite nuts or dried fruits into the melted chocolate to coat, then drop by teaspoonfuls onto waxed paper and chill till firm.

Peanut Butter Bonbons

These candies, pictured on page 20, also can be rolled in cocoa powder—

2	cups sifted powdered sugar
1	cup chopped peanuts
½	cup graham cracker crumbs
¾	cup peanut butter
½	cup butter *or* margarine
1½	pounds dipping chocolate

In a medium mixing bowl combine powdered sugar, peanuts, and graham cracker crumbs. In a small saucepan melt together peanut butter and butter or margarine over low heat, stirring occasionally. Pour peanut butter mixture over dry ingredients in mixing bowl. Stir till moistened. Shape the mixture into 1-inch rounds or ovals. Melt the dipping chocolate; dip the peanut butter balls in the melted chocolate (see melting and dipping instructions on page 34). Store the candies, tightly covered, in a cool, dry place. Makes about 48 chocolate-dipped candies.

Coconut Creams

These candies, resembling miniature candy bars, are pictured on page 20—

1	3-ounce package cream cheese, softened
⅓	cup sifted powdered sugar
1	teaspoon vanilla
1	cup flaked coconut
½	cup finely chopped nuts
1	pound dipping chocolate

In a small mixing bowl stir together softened cream cheese, sifted powdered sugar, and vanilla till well combined. Stir in flaked coconut and chopped nuts. Chill the mixture about 1 hour. Shape into 1-inch rounds or ovals. Melt the dipping chocolate; dip coconut balls in the melted chocolate (see melting and dipping instructions on page 34). Cover and store the candies in a cool, dry place. Makes about 24 chocolate-dipped candies.

Chocolate-Covered Cherries

These gift-giving candies are pictured on page 20—

60 maraschino cherries with
  stems (about two
  10-ounce jars)
3 tablespoons butter *or*
  margarine, softened
3 tablespoons light corn syrup
2 cups sifted powdered sugar
1½ pounds dipping chocolate

Drain the maraschino cherries on paper toweling for several hours or overnight. In a small mixing bowl combine the softened butter or margarine and light corn syrup. Stir in the sifted powdered sugar; knead till the mixture is smooth (chill the mixture if it is too soft to handle). Shape about ½ *teaspoon* of the powdered sugar mixture around *each* maraschino cherry. Place the coated cherries on a waxed-paper-lined baking sheet; chill.

Melt the dipping chocolate (see melting instructions on page 34). Holding the cherries by the stems, dip the cherries, one at a time, in the melted chocolate; spoon chocolate over the cherries to coat. (Be sure to completely seal the cherries in chocolate; otherwise, cherry juice may leak out near the stem after the chocolate has set.) Let excess chocolate drip off cherries. Place the chocolate-covered cherries, stem side up, on a waxed-paper-lined baking sheet. Chill the dipped cherries till the chocolate is firm. Place the cherries in a covered container and let them ripen in the refrigerator for 1 to 2 weeks before serving (ripening is necessary to allow the powdered sugar mixture around the cherries to soften and liquefy). Store cherries in the refrigerator. Makes 60 chocolate-dipped cherries.

Chocolate Truffles

Typically, these rich chocolate candies are irregularly shaped—

6 squares (6 ounces)
  semisweet chocolate,
  coarsely chopped
¼ cup butter *or* margarine
3 tablespoons whipping cream
1 beaten egg yolk
3 tablespoons desired liquor,
  such as rum, Irish
  whiskey, *or* brandy*
1½ pounds dipping chocolate

In a heavy medium saucepan combine the semisweet chocolate, butter or margarine, and whipping cream. Cook and stir over low heat till chocolate is melted, stirring constantly. Gradually stir about half of the hot mixture into the egg yolk. Return all of the mixture to the saucepan. Cook and stir over medium heat for 2 minutes. Remove from heat. Stir in desired liquor. Transfer chocolate mixture to a small mixer bowl; chill about 1 hour or till mixture is completely cool and is smooth, stirring occasionally. Beat the cooled chocolate mixture on medium speed of an electric mixer till slightly fluffy. Chill about 15 minutes more or till mixture holds its shape. Drop from a level teaspoon onto a waxed-paper-lined baking sheet. Chill about 30 minutes more or till firm. Melt the dipping chocolate; dip the candies in the melted chocolate (see melting and dipping instructions on page 34). Makes about 48 chocolate-dipped candies.

Note: For nonalcoholic truffles, prepare the Chocolate Truffles as directed above, *except* substitute 3 tablespoons additional *whipping cream* for the liquor.

Coffee Creams

2 cups sugar
½ cup water
¼ cup light cream
1 tablespoon instant coffee
  crystals
1 tablespoon light corn syrup
½ teaspoon vanilla
1½ pounds dipping chocolate

In a heavy 1½-quart saucepan combine sugar, water, cream, coffee crystals, and corn syrup. Cook and stir over medium heat about 10 minutes or till sugar dissolves and mixture comes to boiling. Continue cooking to 240° (soft-ball stage), stirring only as necessary to prevent sticking (mixture should boil gently over entire surface). Cool, without stirring, to 110° or lukewarm (should take 35 to 40 minutes). Add vanilla. Beat 10 minutes or till smooth.

Shape into ¾-inch rounds or ovals. Place on a waxed-paper-lined baking sheet. Let stand at room temperature about 20 minutes or till dry. Melt dipping chocolate; dip in the melted chocolate (see melting and dipping instructions on page 34). Makes about 56 chocolate-dipped candies.

Chocolate-Dipped Fondant

This basic filling for chocolate-dipped candies can be varied in many ways—

2 cups sugar
1½ cups water
2 tablespoons light corn syrup
  or ⅛ teaspoon cream of
  tartar
1½ pounds dipping chocolate

Butter the sides of a heavy 1½-quart saucepan. In it combine sugar, water, and corn syrup or cream of tartar. Cook and stir over medium heat till sugar dissolves and mixture comes to boiling. Cover and cook for 30 seconds. Uncover; continue to cook to 240° (soft-ball stage) for 20 to 25 minutes without stirring (mixture should boil gently over entire surface). Cooking to 240° should take 20 to 25 minutes. Immediately pour onto a platter. *Do not scrape pan.* Cool for 45 to 50 minutes or till candy feels slightly warm to the touch; do not stir candy during cooling.

Scrape candy toward the center; beat vigorously till the candy is creamy and stiff (should take 5 to 6 minutes). Knead the candy till smooth (should take about 2 minutes). Form into a ball. Wrap in clear plastic wrap; let ripen for 24 hours at room temperature.

Prepare Fondant Mint Patties or Fondant Coconut Drops. Melt chocolate; dip the candy in chocolate (see melting and dipping instructions on page 34). Makes 36 chocolate-dipped patties or 48 chocolate-dipped drops.

Fondant Mint Patties: Prepare Fondant as above. Heat and stir ripened fondant in the top of a double boiler over hot, not boiling, water just till melted and smooth. Remove double boiler from heat, leaving fondant over the hot water. Stir in 1 tablespoon softened *butter or margarine,* ¼ teaspoon *oil of peppermint or oil of cinnamon,* and a few drops *food coloring,* if desired. Drop mixture from a teaspoon onto waxed paper, swirling tops.

Fondant Coconut Drops: Prepare Fondant as directed above. Heat and stir ripened fondant in the top of a double boiler over hot, not boiling, water till melted and smooth. Remove double boiler from heat, leaving fondant over the hot water. Stir in 1 tablespoon softened *butter or margarine* till combined. Stir in 2½ cups *shredded coconut.* Form mixture into ¾-inch balls. Press a whole unblanched *almond* in the center of each ball.

CHOCOLATE

Pies & Pastries

Marble-Top Chocolate-Rum Pie

The light, fluffy filling is also great to layer in parfait glasses—

Pastry for Single-Crust Pie
(see recipe, page 43)
⅓ cup sugar
1 envelope unflavored gelatin
1 cup milk
1 4-ounce package German
    sweet cooking chocolate,
    coarsely chopped
2 beaten egg yolks
¼ cup rum
2 egg whites
¼ cup sugar
1 cup whipping cream
1 tablespoon rum

Prepare and roll out Pastry for Single-Crust Pie. Line a 9-inch pie plate. Trim to ½ inch beyond edge. Flute edge; prick pastry. Bake in a 450° oven for 10 to 12 minutes or till golden. Cool thoroughly on a wire rack.

For the filling, in a saucepan combine the ⅓ cup sugar and unflavored gelatin. Stir in milk and chocolate. Cook and stir till chocolate is melted and mixture is thickened and bubbly. Gradually stir about *1 cup* of the hot mixture into the beaten egg yolks. Return mixture to the saucepan; bring to a gentle boil. Cook and stir 2 minutes more. Remove from heat. Stir in the ¼ cup rum. Chill to the consistency of corn syrup.

Immediately beat the egg whites on medium speed of electric mixer till soft peaks form (tips curl over). Gradually add the ¼ cup sugar, beating on high speed of electric mixer till stiff peaks form (tips stand straight). When the chocolate-gelatin mixture is the consistency of unbeaten egg whites (partially set), fold in the stiff-beaten egg whites. Whip cream and the 1 tablespoon rum till soft peaks form. Alternately layer the chocolate-gelatin mixture and the whipped cream in the baked pastry shell, ending with whipped cream. Use a knife or narrow spatula to gently swirl through the top layers to marble. Chill several hours or till firm. Cover and chill to store. Makes 8 servings.

Banana-Fudge Chiffon Pie

Pastry for Single-Crust Pie
(see recipe, page 43)
1 envelope unflavored gelatin
¼ cup cold water
3 egg yolks
⅓ cup sugar
1 teaspoon vanilla
2 squares (2 ounces)
    unsweetened chocolate,
    coarsely chopped
½ cup water
3 egg whites
½ cup sugar
2 medium bananas, sliced
    ¼ inch thick, *or* 2 cups
    cut-up desired fresh fruit

Prepare and roll out the Pastry for Single-Crust Pie. Line a 9-inch pie plate. Trim the pastry to ½ inch beyond the edge of the pie plate. Flute edge; prick pastry. Bake in a 450° oven for 10 to 12 minutes or till golden. Cool thoroughly on a wire rack.

Soften the gelatin in ¼ cup cold water. In a small mixer bowl beat the egg yolks on high speed of an electric mixer about 5 minutes or till thick and lemon colored. Gradually beat in ⅓ cup sugar; stir in vanilla. In a saucepan combine chocolate and the ½ cup water. Cook and stir over low heat till the chocolate is melted. Add the softened gelatin; stir to dissolve gelatin. Gradually beat the gelatin mixture into the egg yolk mixture. Chill to the consistency of corn syrup, stirring occasionally.

Immediately beat the egg whites on medium speed of electric mixer till soft peaks form (tips curl over). Gradually add the ½ cup sugar, beating on high speed of electric mixer till stiff peaks form (tips stand straight). When the chocolate-gelatin mixture is the consistency of unbeaten egg whites (partially set), fold in stiff-beaten egg whites. Chill till mixture mounds when spooned. Line baked pastry shell with sliced bananas or desired fruit; spread chilled chocolate-gelatin mixture atop. Chill several hours or till firm. Cover and chill to store. Makes 8 servings.

Pictured opposite: Marble-Top Chocolate-Rum Pie

Black Bottom Pie

The "black bottom" is the creamy chocolate layer under the fluffy chiffon—

Pastry for Single-Crust Pie
(see recipe, page 43)
½ cup sugar
1 tablespoon cornstarch
2 cups milk
4 slightly beaten egg yolks
1 teaspoon vanilla
1 6-ounce package (1 cup)
   semisweet chocolate
   pieces
1 envelope unflavored gelatin
¼ cup cold water
1 tablespoon rum *or* ¼
   teaspoon rum extract
4 egg whites
⅓ cup sugar
   Pecan halves

Prepare and roll out Pastry for Single-Crust Pie. Line a 9-inch pie plate. Trim to ½ inch beyond edge of pie plate. Flute edge; prick pastry. Bake in a 450° oven for 10 to 12 minutes or till golden. Cool thoroughly on a wire rack.

In a saucepan combine the ½ cup sugar and cornstarch. Gradually stir in milk. Cook and stir over medium heat till thickened and bubbly. Reduce heat; cook and stir 2 minutes more. Gradually stir about *1 cup* of the hot mixture into yolks. Return to remaining hot mixture in saucepan; bring to a gentle boil. Cook and stir 2 minutes more. Remove from heat. Stir in vanilla. Stir chocolate into *1¼ cups* of the thickened mixture till melted; pour into baked pastry shell. Chill till just set.

Meanwhile, in a 1-cup glass measure soften gelatin in cold water for 5 minutes. Place the cup in a small saucepan containing about 1 inch of water; heat over low heat, stirring to dissolve the gelatin. Stir dissolved gelatin into the remaining hot thickened mixture. Stir in rum or rum extract. Transfer to a medium mixing bowl. Chill to the consistency of corn syrup, stirring occasionally.

Immediately beat egg whites on medium speed of electric mixer till soft peaks form (tips curl over). Gradually add the ⅓ cup sugar, beating on high speed of electric mixer till stiff peaks form (tips stand straight). When the gelatin mixture is the consistency of unbeaten egg whites (partially set), fold into stiff-beaten egg whites. Chill till mixture mounds when spooned. Spread over the chocolate mixture in the baked pastry shell. Chill several hours or till firm. Garnish with pecan halves. Cover and chill to store. Makes 8 servings.

Triple-Tier Chocolate Pie

The pastry, meringue shell, and fluffy chocolate filling are triple treats—

Pastry for Single-Crust Pie
(see recipe, page 43)
3 egg whites
½ teaspoon vinegar
¼ teaspoon ground cinnamon
½ cup sugar
½ of a 16-ounce package
   (30) marshmallows
1 cup milk
1 cup whipping cream
2 squares (2 ounces)
   unsweetened chocolate,
   coarsely chopped
⅛ teaspoon salt
1 teaspoon vanilla
½ cup chopped walnuts

Prepare and roll out Pastry for Single-Crust Pie. Line a 9-inch pie plate. Trim to ½ inch beyond edge. Flute edge; prick pastry. Bake in a 450° oven for 10 to 12 minutes or till golden. Cool thoroughly on a wire rack.

For the meringue shell, in a small mixer bowl combine egg whites, vinegar, and cinnamon. Beat on medium speed of electric mixer till soft peaks form (tips curl over). Gradually add sugar, beating on high speed till stiff peaks form (tips stand straight). Spread over the bottom and up the sides of baked pastry shell. Bake in a 325° oven for 15 minutes. Remove from oven; cool on wire rack.

Meanwhile, for the filling, heat marshmallows, milk, *¼ cup* of the whipping cream, chocolate, and salt till the marshmallows and chocolate are just melted. Stir in vanilla; cool without stirring. Beat remaining whipping cream to soft peaks. Fold the whipped cream and nuts into the chocolate mixture. Chill till the mixture mounds when spooned. Turn into the baked meringue shell. Chill till firm. Cover and chill to store. Makes 8 servings.

Egg-Beating Basics

The trick to beating egg whites successfully is knowing how much to beat them. Most recipes refer to two critical stages: soft peaks and stiff peaks.

When beating egg whites to the soft-peak stage, beat on medium speed of electric mixer till the foam turns white and the tips of the peaks bend in soft curls when the beaters are removed. Gradually add any sugar to the egg whites after soft peaks form.

With additional beating, the foam continues to thicken, becomes even whiter, and forms glossy peaks that stand straight when the beaters are removed. This is the stiff-peak stage, which forms fairly quickly after the soft-peak stage. The egg whites at the stiff-peak stage contain all of the air they are capable of holding. At this point, do not overbeat. Further beating will produce dry, brittle peaks and reduced volume.

Chocolate Marble Pumpkin Pie

You can substitute pumpkin pie spice for the cinnamon, ginger, and cloves—

Pastry for Single-Crust Pie
  (see recipe, page 43)
1   4½-ounce package
      custard dessert mix
⅓   cup sugar
1   teaspoon ground cinnamon
½   teaspoon ground ginger
¼   teaspoon ground cloves
1   16-ounce can (2 cups)
      pumpkin
⅔   cup milk
1   5⅓-ounce can (⅔ cup)
      evaporated milk
½   cup semisweet
      chocolate pieces
1   tablespoon shortening
¼   cup chopped pecans,
      toasted

Prepare and roll out Pastry for Single-Crust Pie. Line a 9-inch pie plate. Trim the pastry to ½ inch beyond the edge of the pie plate. Flute edge; prick pastry. Bake in a 450° oven for 10 to 12 minutes or till golden. Cool thoroughly on a wire rack.

For the filling, in a medium saucepan combine the custard mix, sugar, cinnamon, ginger, and cloves. Stir in pumpkin, milk, and evaporated milk. Cook and stir till bubbly; remove from heat. Cool 10 minutes. Pour *half* of the pumpkin mixture into the baked pastry shell. Melt together the chocolate pieces and shortening (see instructions on page 4); stir into ½ *cup* of the pumpkin mixture till well combined. Carefully pour the chocolate mixture over the pumpkin mixture in pastry shell. Top with remaining pumpkin mixture. With a knife or a narrow spatula, gently swirl through layers to marble. Sprinkle with toasted chopped pecans. Cover; chill several hours or till firm. Chill to store. Makes 8 servings.

How To Make Chocolate Marble Pumpkin Pie

Pour *half* of the pumpkin mixture into pastry shell. Pour chocolate mixture atop pumpkin mixture. Top with the remaining pumpkin mixture. With a knife or a narrow spatula, gently swirl through the layers to marble, as shown in the photo.

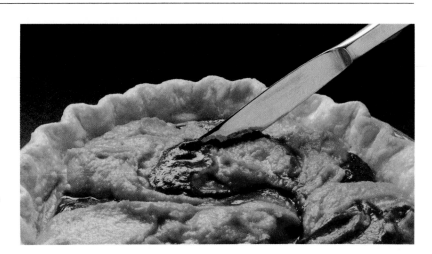

Milk Chocolate Pecan Pie

The chocolate pieces rise to the top of the pie when baked—

Pastry for Single-Crust Pie
    (see recipe, page 43)
3   eggs
1   cup light corn syrup
⅔   cup sugar
⅓   cup butter *or* margarine,
        melted
1   cup chopped pecans
½   cup milk chocolate
        pieces

Prepare and roll out Pastry for Single-Crust Pie. Line a 9-inch pie plate. Trim pastry to ½ inch beyond edge of pie plate. Flute edge; *do not prick* pastry. Set aside.

For the filling, in a medium mixing bowl beat the eggs slightly with a rotary beater or fork. Stir in the light corn syrup, sugar, and melted butter or margarine; mix well. Stir in the chopped pecans and milk chocolate pieces. Place the pie shell on the oven rack; pour the filling into pastry-lined pie plate. To prevent overbrowning, cover the edge of the pie with foil. Bake in a 350° oven for 25 minutes. Remove the foil; bake about 25 minutes more or till a knife inserted near center comes out clean. Cool the pie thoroughly on a wire rack before serving. Cover and chill to store. Makes 8 servings.

Chocolate Cream Pie

Pastry for Single-Crust Pie
    (see recipe, page 43)
¾   cup sugar
⅓   cup cornstarch
2½   cups milk
½   of a 6-ounce package
        (½ cup) semisweet
        chocolate pieces
3   slightly beaten egg yolks
2   tablespoons butter *or*
        margarine, cut up
1½   teaspoons vanilla
3   egg whites
½   teaspoon vanilla
¼   teaspoon cream of tartar
⅓   cup sugar

Prepare and roll out Pastry for Single-Crust Pie. Line a 9-inch pie plate. Trim to ½ inch beyond edge. Flute edge; prick pastry. Bake in a 450° oven for 10 to 12 minutes or till golden. Cool thoroughly on a wire rack.

For the filling, in a saucepan combine the ¾ cup sugar and cornstarch. Gradually stir in milk. Cook and stir till the mixture is thickened and bubbly. Reduce heat; cook and stir 2 minutes more. Stir in the semisweet chocolate pieces; cook and stir till the chocolate is melted. Remove from heat. Gradually stir about *1 cup* hot mixture into the slightly beaten egg yolks. Return the mixture to the saucepan; bring to a gentle boil. Cook and stir 2 minutes more. Stir in butter or margarine and the 1½ teaspoons vanilla. Turn the hot filling into the baked pastry shell.

For the meringue, in a small mixer bowl beat egg whites, the ½ teaspoon vanilla, and cream of tartar on medium speed of electric mixer till soft peaks form (tips curl over). Gradually add the ⅓ cup sugar, beating on high speed of electric mixer till stiff peaks form (tips stand straight). Spread meringue over filling; seal to edge. Bake in a 350° oven for 12 to 15 minutes or till done; cool. Cover and chill to store. Makes 8 servings.

Meringue-Topped Pies

Meringue-topped pies are best if they are eaten as soon as they are cooled, but you can store them, covered, in a refrigerator. To cover the pies, insert several wooden picks halfway into the meringue. Loosely cover with clear plastic wrap, using picks to hold plastic wrap away from pies. Place pies in the refrigerator. (Refrigeration will cause the meringue to become somewhat rubbery.) Before cutting a meringue-topped pie, dip the blade of the knife in water to prevent sticking (don't dry the knife). Repeat dipping the knife in water whenever the meringue begins to stick.

French Silk Pie

Pastry for Single-Crust Pie
(see recipe, below)
3 squares (3 ounces)
unsweetened chocolate
1 cup sugar
¾ cup butter (not margarine)
1½ teaspoons vanilla
3 eggs
Unsweetened whipped cream
Chocolate Curls (see
instructions, page 90)

Prepare and roll out Pastry for Single-Crust Pie. Line a 9-inch pie plate. Trim pastry to ½ inch beyond edge. Flute edge; prick pastry. Bake in a 450° oven for 10 to 12 minutes or till golden. Cool thoroughly. Meanwhile, melt chocolate (see instructions on page 4); cool.

In a small mixer bowl beat together sugar and butter about 4 minutes or till light and fluffy. Beat in melted chocolate and vanilla. Add eggs, one at a time, beating on medium speed of an electric mixer for 2 minutes after each addition and scraping sides of bowl constantly. Turn into baked pastry shell. Chill several hours or overnight till set. Garnish with whipped cream and Chocolate Curls. Cover and chill to store. Makes 10 servings.

Note: Some brands of margarine produce a nonfluffy, sticky filling when used in this pie. The results were so unsatisfactory that we recommend using only butter.

SHORT & SWEET

Quick Chocolate Pie

Dessert topping, chocolate frosting, and cream cheese make the filling—

1 1½-ounce envelope dessert
topping mix
½ of a 16½-ounce can
(about 1 cup)
chocolate frosting
1 3-ounce package cream
cheese, softened
1 9-inch graham cracker
pie shell
Chopped peanuts (optional)

In a small mixer bowl prepare dessert topping mix according to package directions; transfer to another bowl. In same mixer bowl beat chocolate frosting and cream cheese till fluffy. Fold in whipped topping. Turn into graham cracker pie shell. Chill several hours or overnight. Before serving, sprinkle with chopped peanuts, if desired. Cover and chill to store. Makes 8 servings.

Pastry for Single-Crust Pie

1¼ cups all-purpose flour
½ teaspoon salt
⅓ cup shortening *or* lard
3 to 4 tablespoons cold water

In a bowl stir together flour and salt. Cut in shortening or lard till pieces are the size of small peas. Sprinkle *1 tablespoon* of the water over part of mixture; gently toss with a fork. Push to side of bowl. Repeat with remaining water till all is moistened. Form dough into a ball.

On a lightly floured surface flatten dough with hands. Roll dough from center to edge, forming a circle about 12 inches in diameter. Wrap pastry around rolling pin. Unroll onto a 9-inch pie plate, being careful to avoid stretching the pastry. Trim pastry to ½ inch beyond the edge of the pie plate. Make a fluted, rope-shaped, or scalloped edge.

For a baked pie shell, prick bottom and sides with fork. Bake in a 450° oven for 10 to 12 minutes. (*Or,* line pastry with foil and fill with dry beans, or line pastry with a double thickness of heavy-duty foil; bake for 5 minutes. Remove beans and foil or heavy-duty foil; bake for 5 to 7 minutes more or till golden.) Makes one 9-inch pastry shell.

Cherry-Topped Chocolate Cream Puffs

1   cup all-purpose flour
1   tablespoon sugar
¼   teaspoon salt
½   cup butter *or* margarine
1   square (1 ounce) semisweet chocolate
1   cup water
4   eggs
½   cup sugar
2   tablespoons cornstarch
¼   teaspoon salt
2   cups milk
2   beaten egg yolks *or* 1 beaten egg
2   tablespoons butter *or* margarine, cut up
1½   teaspoons vanilla
1   21-ounce can cherry pie filling
    Chocolate-flavored syrup (optional)

For chocolate cream puffs, stir together flour, the 1 tablespoon sugar, and ¼ teaspoon salt. Set aside. In a medium saucepan melt the ½ cup butter and chocolate over low heat. Add water; bring to boil. Add flour mixture to chocolate mixture all at once. Stir vigorously. Cook and stir till mixture forms a ball that doesn't separate. Remove from heat; cool slightly (about 5 minutes). Add 4 eggs, one at a time, beating with a wooden spoon for 1 to 2 minutes, or till smooth, after each addition.

Drop the batter by heaping tablespoonfuls 3 inches apart onto a greased baking sheet. Bake in a 400° oven for 35 to 40 minutes or till puffy. Remove from oven; split and remove soft dough inside. Cool on a wire rack.

Meanwhile, in a heavy medium saucepan combine the ½ cup sugar, cornstarch, and the ¼ teaspoon salt. Stir in milk. Cook and stir over medium heat till thickened and bubbly; cook and stir 2 minutes more. Gradually stir about *1 cup* of the hot mixture into the 2 beaten egg yolks *or* 1 beaten egg. Return all the mixture to the saucepan. Cook and stir 2 minutes more. Remove from heat. Stir in the 2 tablespoons butter or margarine and the vanilla just till butter melts. Pour mixture into a bowl. Cover surface with clear plastic wrap. Cool, then chill without stirring. Spoon into bottom half of each cream puff. Top with cherry pie filling and the cream puff top. Drizzle with chocolate-flavored syrup, if desired. Makes 10 servings.

Note: Cream puffs are leavened by steam and may collapse when removed from the oven. Prevent cream puffs from collapsing by immediately splitting each cream puff and removing the soft dough inside.

Chocolate Fried Pies

½   cup sugar
¼   cup all-purpose flour
1   tablespoon unsweetened cocoa powder
½   cup milk
2   tablespoons butter *or* margarine
½   teaspoon vanilla
2   cups packaged biscuit mix
½   cup milk
    Cooking oil for shallow-fat frying
    Sifted powdered sugar

For the filling, in a saucepan combine sugar, flour, and unsweetened cocoa powder. Stir in ½ cup milk and butter or margarine. Cook and stir over medium heat till the mixture is thickened and bubbly. Cook and stir 1 minute more. Stir in vanilla. Cool.

For the dough, in a mixing bowl stir together the biscuit mix and ½ cup milk. On a well-floured surface knead the dough 12 strokes. Roll the dough to slightly less than ⅛-inch thickness. Cut dough into twelve 4-inch circles. Reroll as necessary. Place about 1 tablespoon filling in the center of each circle of dough. Brush the edge of the dough with water. Fold the dough over the filling; press the edges together with tines of a fork to seal. In a skillet heat 1 inch cooking oil to 375°. Fry the pastries, several at a time, about 2 minutes or till golden, turning once. Drain on paper toweling. Sprinkle warm pastries with sifted powdered sugar. Makes 12 servings.

Pictured opposite: Danish pastry and croissant versions of Chocolate Puff Pastry (see recipe, page 46)

Chocolate Puff Pastry

These flaky, rich pastries are pictured on page 44—

1 *or* 1½ cups butter *or*
    margarine*
⅓ cup all-purpose flour
2 packages active dry yeast
½ cup warm water (110°
    to 115°)
¾ cup milk
3 squares (3 ounces)
    semisweet chocolate
¼ cup sugar
1 teaspoon salt
1 egg
3¾ to 4¼ cups all-purpose flour
    Chocolate-Almond Filling *or*
    Chocolate-Orange Filling
1 egg yolk (optional)
1 tablespoon milk (optional)

*For Danish pastries use 1 cup butter; for croissants use 1½ cups butter. Beat together butter and ⅓ cup flour. Roll mixture between 2 sheets of waxed paper into a 12x6-inch rectangle. Chill at least 1 hour. Soften yeast in warm water. Heat and stir ¾ cup milk, chocolate, sugar, and salt till sugar dissolves and chocolate melts. Cool to lukewarm (115° to 120°). Turn into a large mixer bowl. Add softened yeast and egg; beat well. Stir in *2 cups* of the flour; beat well. Using a spoon, stir in as much remaining flour as you can. On lightly floured surface knead in enough remaining flour to make a moderately soft dough that is smooth and elastic (3 to 5 minutes total). Cover; let rest 10 minutes.

Roll dough into a 14-inch square. Place chilled butter on half of dough. Fold over other half; seal edges. Roll into a 21x12-inch rectangle. Fold into thirds; seal edges. Chill dough about 30 minutes. Roll into a 21x12-inch rectangle. Fold and roll twice more, chilling after each folding. Fold into thirds to form a 12x7-inch rectangle. Chill several hours or overnight.

To make Danish pastries, prepare Chocolate-Almond Filling. Divide dough crosswise into thirds; chill portions till ready to use. For rectangular pastries, roll ⅓ of the dough at a time into a 9x6-inch rectangle. Cut into 3x2-inch rectangles; place on ungreased baking sheet. Make a thumbprint in center of each rectangle; fill with 1 rounded teaspoonful filling. For bunting pastries, roll ⅓ of the dough at a time into a 9x6-inch rectangle. Cut into 3-inch squares. Place on ungreased baking sheet. Spoon 1 rounded teaspoonful filling in center of each square. Bring 2 opposite corners to center; seal.

For both shapes, cover and let rise till nearly double (45 to 60 minutes). Bake in a 450° oven for 8 to 10 minutes or till lightly browned. If desired, drizzle with Confectioner's Icing (see recipe, page 77). Serve warm with butter, if desired. Makes 27 rectangular or 18 bunting pastries.

To make croissants, prepare Chocolate-Orange Filling. Cut dough crosswise into fourths. Roll each fourth into a 12-inch circle. Cut each circle into 8 wedges. Place 1 tablespoonful filling at the base of each wedge. Roll up loosely, starting at base. Place point down on ungreased baking sheets; curve ends. Cover; let rise till nearly double (45 to 60 minutes). Beat egg yolk and 1 tablespoon milk; brush over pastries, if desired. Bake in a 375° oven for 12 to 15 minutes or till lightly browned. Makes 32.

Chocolate-Almond Filling: Melt 2 squares (2 ounces) *unsweetened chocolate* (see instructions on page 4). Beat 1 cup sifted *powdered sugar* and ¼ cup *butter* till fluffy. Beat in chocolate; stir in ½ cup chopped toasted *almonds.*

Chocolate-Orange Filling: Combine 1 cup *sugar,* 3 tablespoons *cornstarch,* and ¼ teaspoon *salt.* Stir in 1⅓ cups *orange juice* and 4 squares (4 ounces) *unsweetened chocolate,* coarsely chopped. Cook and stir till chocolate melts and mixture bubbles. Cook and stir 2 minutes more.

How To Make Chocolate Puff Pastry

The flakiness of the puff pastry is achieved by incorporating butter into the dough. To do this, roll the dough into a 14-inch square. Place the chilled butter on half of the dough. Bring the other half of the dough up over the butter, as shown in the photo; seal edges.

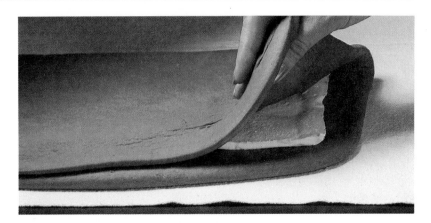

After sealing in the butter, roll the dough into a 21x12-inch rectangle. Gently lift the dough, without stretching, and fold it into thirds, as shown in the photo. Seal the edges together. Then chill the dough about 30 minutes to allow the butter to resolidify.

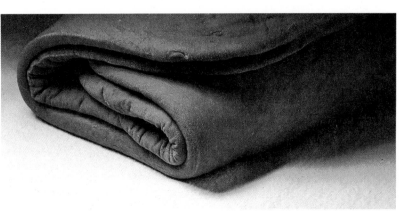

To shape bunting rolls for the Danish pastries, place 1 rounded teaspoonful Chocolate-Almond Filling in the center of each 3-inch square of dough. Bring 2 opposite corners of the dough to the center. Press the corners together to seal. If you like, you may insert a wooden pick through the center to ensure a firm seal.

To make the croissants, place 1 tablespoonful Chocolate-Orange Filling at the base of each wedge of dough. Roll up the dough loosely, starting at the base of the wedge. Place the croissant, point side down, on an ungreased baking sheet. Curve the ends of the croissant.

CHOCOLATE

Tortes
Cheesecakes & Soufflés

Chocolate-Cinnamon Meringue Torte

2 egg whites
½ teaspoon vanilla
¼ teaspoon cream of tartar
¼ teaspoon ground cinnamon
⅔ cup sugar
½ cup all-purpose flour
1 teaspoon baking powder
1 teaspoon ground cinnamon
  Dash salt
1 cup butter *or* margarine
1¼ cups sugar
6 egg yolks
1 cup ground pecans,
  walnuts, *or* almonds
4 squares (4 ounces)
  unsweetened chocolate,
  grated
6 egg whites
  Creamy Chocolate Frosting
  Chocolate Curls (see
  instructions, page 90)

Cover a baking sheet with brown paper. Draw one 8-inch circle on the paper; set aside. For meringue, in a mixer bowl beat 2 egg whites, vanilla, cream of tartar, and ¼ teaspoon cinnamon on medium speed of electric mixer till soft peaks form. Gradually add the ⅔ cup sugar, beating till stiff peaks form. Spoon onto circle on paper, smoothing top and sides with a spatula. Bake in a 300° oven for 1 hour. Turn off heat; let dry in closed oven for 1 hour.

Grease and lightly flour two 9x1½-inch round baking pans. Stir together flour, baking powder, the 1 teaspoon cinnamon, and salt. In a large mixer bowl beat butter on medium speed of electric mixer about 30 seconds. Add the 1¼ cups sugar and beat till fluffy. Beat in egg yolks. Add dry ingredients; beat on low speed till well combined. Stir in nuts and chocolate. Transfer to another large bowl.

Wash beaters and large mixer bowl thoroughly. In large mixer bowl beat 6 egg whites till stiff peaks form. Fold about ¼ of the beaten egg whites into the batter; fold in remaining egg whites. Turn into prepared pans. Bake in a 350° oven for 40 to 45 minutes or till done. Cool 10 minutes on wire racks. Remove from pans; cool thoroughly. Meanwhile, prepare the Creamy Chocolate Frosting.

To assemble, peel paper off meringue. Spread ⅓ of the frosting over bottom cake layer. Place meringue atop. Spread about ⅓ of frosting over meringue layer. Top with second cake layer. Spread with remaining frosting. Garnish with Chocolate Curls. Chill to store. Makes 10 servings.

Creamy Chocolate Frosting: Melt one 6-ounce package *semisweet chocolate pieces* over low heat, stirring constantly; remove from heat. Stir together 2 beaten *egg yolks* and ¼ cup *water*. Stir about *half* of the melted chocolate into egg yolk mixture. Return all to saucepan. Cook and stir about 1 minute more. Cool to room temperature. Beat 1 cup *whipping cream* and ¼ cup *sugar* till soft peaks form. Fold into the chocolate mixture. Cover and chill about 1 hour or till of spreading consistency.

SHORT & SWEET

Brownie-Nut Torte

The brownie mix helps cut preparation time to about 15 minutes—

1 15½-ounce package
  brownie mix
1 cup chopped nuts
1 4-ounce container frozen
  whipped dessert topping,
  thawed
⅓ cup miniature semisweet
  chocolate pieces
1 to 2 tablespoons coffee
  liqueur (optional)

Grease and lightly flour two 8x1½-inch round baking pans. Prepare the brownie mix according to package directions, *except* stir nuts into batter. Turn batter into prepared pans. Bake in a 350° oven about 20 minutes or till a wooden pick inserted in the center comes out clean. Remove from pans; cool thoroughly on wire racks.

Stir together whipped topping, chocolate pieces, and liqueur, if desired. Spread *half* of the topping mixture over bottom brownie layer. Place the second brownie layer atop. Spread with the remaining topping mixture. Chill for 1 hour before serving. Makes 6 to 8 servings.

Pictured opposite: Chocolate-Cinnamon Meringue Torte

Nutty Chocolate Torte Supreme

This rich dessert uses a full 8-ounce package of semisweet chocolate—

½   cup all-purpose flour
1   teaspoon ground cinnamon
1   cup butter *or* margarine
1¼ cups sugar
8   egg yolks
2   cups ground walnuts,
      pecans, *or* almonds
5½ squares (5½ ounces)
      semisweet chocolate,
      grated
8   egg whites
½   cup milk
⅓   cup sugar
2   squares (2 ounces)
      semisweet chocolate,
      coarsely chopped
¼   cup butter *or* margarine,
      cut up
1   teaspoon vanilla
2   cups ground walnuts,
      pecans, *or* almonds
    Chocolate Glaze

Grease and lightly flour three 8x1½-inch round baking pans. Stir together flour and cinnamon. In a large mixer bowl beat 1 cup butter with an electric mixer about 30 seconds. Add the 1¼ cups sugar and beat till fluffy. Add egg yolks, one at a time, beating well on medium speed. Add dry ingredients; beat well. Stir in 2 cups nuts and 5½ ounces grated chocolate. Transfer to another large bowl.

Wash beaters and large mixer bowl thoroughly. In large mixer bowl beat egg whites till stiff peaks form. Fold about ¼ of the egg whites into batter; fold in remaining egg whites. Divide batter evenly among the prepared pans. Bake in a 350° oven for 30 to 35 minutes or till a wooden pick inserted in the center comes out clean. Cool 10 minutes. Remove from pans; cool thoroughly on wire racks.

For filling, in a saucepan combine milk, the ⅓ cup sugar, and the 2 ounces chopped chocolate. Cook and stir till chocolate is melted. Remove from heat. Stir in the ¼ cup butter and vanilla. Stir in 2 cups nuts; cool to room temperature. Spread between torte layers. Spread top with warm Chocolate Glaze. Chill to store. Makes 12 servings.

Chocolate Fudge Glaze: In a small saucepan combine ¼ cup *sugar* and 2 teaspoons *cornstarch*. Stir in ¼ cup *water* and ½ square (½ ounce) *semisweet chocolate*, coarsely chopped. Cook and stir till chocolate is melted and mixture is thickened and bubbly. Cook and stir 2 minutes more. Remove from heat; stir in ½ teaspoon *vanilla.*

Viennese Sacher Torte

This traditional Austrian torte combines chocolate with apricot jam—

1   6-ounce package semisweet
      chocolate pieces
⅔   cup butter *or* margarine
8   slightly beaten egg yolks
1   teaspoon vanilla
8   egg whites
⅔   cup sugar
1   cup all-purpose flour
¼   cup sugar
2   teaspoons cornstarch
⅓   cup water
½   square (½ ounce)
      unsweetened chocolate,
      coarsely chopped
½   teaspoon vanilla
½   cup apricot jam

Grease and lightly flour two 9x1½-inch round baking pans. Melt together chocolate and butter (see instructions on page 4); cool. Stir in egg yolks and 1 teaspoon vanilla; set aside. In a large mixer bowl beat egg whites on medium speed of electric mixer till soft peaks form. Gradually add the ⅔ cup sugar, beating on high speed till stiff peaks form. Stir about ⅓ of the beaten egg whites into the chocolate mixture. Pour the chocolate-egg white mixture over remaining beaten egg whites. Sprinkle flour over all. Carefully fold mixture together; *do not overfold.* Turn batter into prepared pans. Bake in a 350° oven for 20 to 25 minutes or till a wooden pick inserted in the center comes out clean. Cool 10 minutes on wire racks. Remove from pans; cool thoroughly on wire racks.

For the glaze, in a small saucepan combine the ¼ cup sugar and cornstarch. Stir in water. Cook and stir till thickened and bubbly. Cook and stir 2 minutes more. Add the unsweetened chocolate. Cook and stir till chocolate is melted. Remove from heat; stir in ½ teaspoon vanilla. Strain apricot jam. Spread bottom torte layer with jam. Place second layer atop jam. Spread the glaze over torte, allowing some to drip down sides. Makes 8 to 10 servings.

Zagreb Torte

The origin of this rich, moist torte can be traced to Yugoslavia—

5 squares (5 ounces)
    semisweet chocolate
¾ cup butter *or* margarine
⅔ cup sugar
9 egg yolks
2 cups ground filberts
    or walnuts
⅓ cup fine dry bread crumbs
2 tablespoons milk
9 egg whites
    Chocolate Filling
    Chocolate Glaze
    Blanched whole filberts
    or walnut halves

Grease and lightly flour four 8x1½-inch round baking pans. Melt chocolate (see instructions on page 4); cool. In a large mixer bowl beat butter and sugar on medium speed of electric mixer till fluffy. Add egg yolks, one at a time, beating well on medium speed. Stir in chocolate, nuts, bread crumbs, and milk. Transfer to another large bowl.

Thoroughly wash beaters and large mixer bowl. In large mixer bowl beat egg whites on medium speed of electric mixer till stiff peaks form. Fold beaten egg whites into egg yolk mixture; turn into prepared pans. Bake in a 350° oven about 15 minutes or till a wooden pick inserted in the center comes out clean. Cool 10 minutes on wire racks; remove from pans. Cool thoroughly on wire racks.

Prepare Chocolate Filling; spread between torte layers. Next, prepare Chocolate Glaze; immediately spoon over torte, allowing some to drip down the sides. Garnish with whole filberts or walnut halves. Makes 16 to 18 servings.

Chocolate Filling: In a small mixing bowl combine 1 cup sifted *powdered sugar* and 1 tablespoon all-purpose *flour*. In a medium saucepan stir together 4 beaten *egg yolks* and ¼ cup *milk*. Add the dry ingredients to the egg yolk mixture. Cook and stir over medium heat till the mixture is very thick. Remove from heat; stir in 2 tablespoons *crème d'almond, hazelnut liqueur, or maraschino liqueur*, and 1 teaspoon *vanilla*. Cover the surface of the mixture with waxed paper; cool. Melt 3 squares (3 ounces) *semisweet chocolate* (see instructions on page 4); cool. Beat together ½ cup softened *butter or margarine* and melted chocolate. Gradually stir egg yolk mixture into chocolate mixture.

Chocolate Glaze: Melt together 1 square (1 ounce) *unsweetened chocolate* and 1 tablespoon *butter or margarine*. Stir in 1 cup sifted *powdered sugar* and 1 teaspoon *vanilla*. Add enough *hot water* (1 to 2 tablespoons) to make the glaze of pouring consistency.

What is a Torte?

It's sometimes hard to tell the difference between a cake and a torte, but here are some guidelines. European in origin, a torte is basically a layered cake. Today the basis for a torte is a cake (made with little or no flour) or a hard meringue. Bread crumbs or nuts may be substituted for all or some of the flour in the cakes. The only leavening in a torte usually is the air that is incorporated into the eggs. Tortes also customarily have at least two layers, separated by fillings such as icing, custard, fruit, or whipped cream. To create this spectacular dessert, you can start from scratch as with the classic Zagreb Torte, or use convenience products as with the Brownie-Nut Torte on page 49. Either way, you're guaranteed a torte that will be a grand treat for all.

Chocolate-Rum Cheesecake

Serve chilled or bring to room temperature before serving—

1   **12-ounce package semisweet chocolate pieces**
1½ **cups graham cracker crumbs**
2   **tablespoons sugar**
⅓   **cup butter *or* margarine, melted**
2   **8-ounce packages cream cheese, softened**
1   **cup sugar**
¼   **teaspoon salt**
3   **eggs**
2   **8-ounce cartons dairy sour cream**
⅓   **cup rum**
¼   **cup milk**

Melt the semisweet chocolate (see instructions on page 4); cool. For the crust, combine graham cracker crumbs and the 2 tablespoons sugar. Add the melted butter or margarine, stirring till well combined. Press the crumb mixture onto the bottom and 2½ inches up the sides of a 9-inch springform pan.

In a large mixer bowl beat together softened cream cheese, the 1 cup sugar, salt, and melted chocolate just till smooth. Add the eggs; beat on low speed of electric mixer just till combined. *Do not overbeat.* Stir in dairy sour cream, rum, and milk just till combined. Turn the mixture into prepared graham cracker crust. Bake in a 375° oven for 60 to 65 minutes or till a knife inserted near the center comes out almost clean. Cool on a wire rack. Chill the cheesecake for 4 to 5 hours. Before serving, use a knife or a narrow metal spatula to carefully loosen the sides of the cheesecake from the springform pan. Remove the sides of the springform pan. Makes 12 servings.

How To Make Chocolate-Rum Cheesecake

For the crust, press the graham cracker crumb mixture onto the bottom and 2½ inches up the sides of a 9-inch springform pan. Be sure to equally distribute the mixture to ensure that the crust bakes evenly.

Before serving, use a knife or a narrow metal spatula to carefully loosen the sides of the cheesecake from the springform pan. Then remove the sides of the pan, as shown in the photo.

Chocolate Chip-Coffee Cheesecake

Plan to allow about 25 minutes for recipe preparation—

1½ cups milk
 1 tablespoon instant coffee
    crystals
 1 11- *or* 12⅛-ounce
    package cheesecake mix
 1 3-ounce package cream
    cheese, cut up
 1 6-ounce package
    miniature semisweet
    chocolate pieces
    Shaved Chocolate (see
    instuctions, page 90)

In a small saucepan combine milk and coffee crystals. Cook and stir over low heat till coffee crystals are dissolved; set aside. Prepare the crumb crust from the cheesecake mix according to package directions. Press the crumb mixture onto the bottom and 1 inch up the sides of an 8-inch springform pan or a 9-inch pie plate; chill the crust while preparing the filling.

For the filling, in a small mixer bowl combine the cheesecake filling mix, the cut-up cream cheese, and milk mixture. Beat on low speed of electric mixer till combined. Continue beating on medium speed of electric mixer about 3 minutes more or till the cheesecake filling is very thick and smooth. Stir the miniature semisweet chocolate pieces into the cheesecake filling. Pour the cheesecake filling into the prepared crumb crust. Chill at least 1 hour. If using the springform pan, use a knife or narrow spatula to carefully loosen the sides of the cheescake from the springform pan. Remove the sides of the springform pan. Garnish cheesecake with Shaved Chocolate. Makes 10 servings.

No-Bake Chocolate Cheesecake

1¼ cups graham cracker
    crumbs
 ¼ cup sugar
 ¼ cup unsweetened cocoa
    powder
 ½ cup butter *or* margarine,
    melted
 1 envelope unflavored gelatin
 ½ cup cold water
 4 squares (4 ounces)
    unsweetened chocolate
 1 14-ounce can (1¼ cups)
    Eagle Brand sweetened
    condensed milk
 2 8-ounce packages cream
    cheese, softened
 ½ teaspoon almond extract
 1 8-ounce container frozen
    whipped dessert topping,
    thawed
    Sweetened sliced
    strawberries *or*
    peaches, *or* canned
    cherry pie filling
    (optional)

For the crust, combine graham cracker crumbs, sugar, and cocoa powder. Add the melted butter or margarine, stirring till well combined. Press crumb mixture onto the bottom and 1¾ inches up the sides of a 9-inch springform pan. Chill the crust while preparing the filling.

For the filling, in a 1-cup glass measure soften the gelatin in cold water. Place the cup in a saucepan containing about 1 inch water; cook and stir over low heat till gelatin is dissolved. Remove saucepan from heat. Melt chocolate (see instructions on page 4); cool. Stir together sweetened condensed milk, dissolved gelatin, and melted chocolate. In a large mixer bowl beat the cream cheese and almond extract on medium speed of electric mixer till smooth. Gradually add the chocolate mixture and beat till light and fluffy. Fold in whipped topping. Turn into prepared crust. Chill at least 6 hours or overnight. Before serving, use a knife or a narrow metal spatula to carefully loosen the sides of the cheesecake from the springform pan. Remove the sides of the springform pan. Top cheesecake with sliced strawberries, sliced peaches, or canned cherry pie filling, if desired. Makes 12 servings.

Crème de Menthe Cheesecake

2 cups finely crushed
    chocolate wafers (about
    38 cookies)
½ cup butter *or* margarine,
    melted
2 8-ounce packages cream
    cheese, softened
1 cup sugar
⅓ cup green crème de menthe
3 eggs
3 8-ounce cartons dairy
    sour cream
4 squares (4 ounces)
    semisweet chocolate
½ cup dairy sour cream

For the crust, combine the crushed chocolate wafers and melted butter or margarine. Stir till well combined. Press the chocolate crumb mixture onto the bottom and 2 inches up the sides of a 9-inch springform pan or 2½ inches up the sides of an 8-inch springform pan.

For the filling, in a large mixer bowl beat together cream cheese, sugar, and crème de menthe just till smooth. Add eggs; beat on low speed of electric mixer just till combined. *Do not overbeat.* Stir in the 3 cartons sour cream. Turn into prepared crust. Bake in a 375° oven for 55 to 60 minutes for the 9-inch cheesecake, or about 65 minutes for the 8-inch cheesecake, or till a knife inserted near the center comes out almost clean. Cool on a wire rack. While cheesecake is cooling, melt chocolate (see instructions on page 4); cool for 5 minutes. Stir the ½ cup sour cream into melted chocolate. Spread over warm cheesecake. Chill for 4 to 5 hours. Before serving, use a knife or a narrow metal spatula to carefully loosen sides of cheesecake from springform pan. Remove the sides of the springform pan. Makes 12 servings.

Chocolate-Covered Marble Cheesecake

A hint of orange makes this marbled dessert extra special—

1½ cups finely crushed vanilla
    wafers (about 33 cookies)
⅓ cup butter *or* margarine,
    melted
2 squares (2 ounces)
    semisweet chocolate
2 8-ounce packages cream
    cheese, softened
1 cup cream-style cottage
    cheese, drained
¼ cup milk
1 teaspoon finely shredded
    orange peel
1 teaspoon vanilla
1 cup sugar
2 tablespoons all-purpose
    flour
⅛ teaspoon salt
2 eggs
1 egg yolk
4 squares (4 ounces)
    semisweet chocolate
4 teaspoons shortening
    Halved orange slices *or*
    mandarin oranges
    (optional)
    Finely shredded orange peel
    (optional)

For the crust, combine the crushed wafers and melted butter or margarine. Stir till well combined. Press crumb mixture onto the bottom and 1¾ inches up the sides of an 8-inch springform pan.

For the filling, melt the 2 squares semisweet chocolate (see instructions on page 4); cool. In a large mixer bowl beat together cream cheese, cottage cheese, milk, 1 teaspoon orange peel, and vanilla till well combined. Stir together the 1 cup sugar, flour, and salt; gradually beat into cheese mixture. Add the 2 eggs and egg yolk all at once; beat on low speed of electric mixer just till combined. *Do not overbeat.* Transfer *half* of the cheese mixture (about 2 cups) to another bowl. To the remaining mixture, stir in the melted chocolate till well combined. Spoon filling into the prepared crust, alternating light and dark mixtures. Using a narrow spatula, swirl gently through the filling to marble. Bake in a 450° oven for 10 minutes. Reduce heat to 300°; bake about 40 minutes more or till a knife inserted near center comes out almost clean. Cool on a wire rack. While cheesecake is cooling, melt together the 4 squares semisweet chocolate and shortening. Spread over warm cheesecake. Chill 4 to 5 hours. Before serving, use a knife or a narrow metal spatula to carefully loosen sides of cheesecake from springform pan. Remove the sides of the springform pan. Garnish cheesecake with a ring of halved orange slices or mandarin oranges and finely shredded orange peel, if desired. Makes 12 servings.

Pictured opposite: Crème de Menthe Cheesecake

Mini Chocolate Soufflés with Caramel-Pecan Sauce

Mix these individual soufflés right in your blender—

¾ cup semisweet chocolate
    pieces
4 eggs
1 egg white
⅓ cup milk
¼ cup sugar
1 8-ounce package cream
    cheese, cubed
    Caramel-Pecan Sauce

Melt semisweet chocolate pieces (see instructions on page 4); cool. In a blender container combine eggs, egg white, milk, and sugar. Cover; blend till smooth. With the blender running, add the cream cheese cubes through the opening in the blender lid or with the lid slightly ajar; blend till smooth. Add the melted chocolate; cover and blend just till combined. Pour the chocolate mixture into four *ungreased* 1-cup soufflé dishes. Bake in a 375° oven about 35 minutes or till set. Serve at once with the warm Caramel-Pecan Sauce. Makes 4 servings.

Caramel-Pecan Sauce: In a small saucepan combine ¼ cup packed *brown sugar* and 1½ teaspoons *cornstarch*. Stir in ⅓ cup *milk* and 1 tablespoon *light corn syrup*. Cook and stir till the mixture is thickened and bubbly. Cook and stir 2 minutes more. (The mixture may appear curdled during cooking.) Stir in 2 tablespoons coarsely chopped *pecans*, 1 tablespoon *butter or margarine*, and 2 teaspoons *rum or brandy*. Remove the sauce from heat; cover surface with clear plastic wrap. Cool slightly.

Chilled Chocolate Soufflé

You'll delight in the flavor of this cool chocolate-coconut dessert—

4 squares (4 ounces)
    semisweet chocolate
¼ cup sugar
1 envelope unflavored gelatin
1⅓ cups milk
4 beaten egg yolks
⅓ cup cream of coconut
1 teaspoon vanilla
4 egg whites
2 tablespoons sugar
½ cup whipping cream
    Unsweetened whipped cream
¼ cup coconut, toasted

For the collar, fold a 21-inch-long piece of waxed paper or foil lengthwise into thirds; butter one side. Attach paper or foil, buttered side in, around the outside of a 1-quart soufflé dish so that the paper extends 1 inch above dish. Melt the chocolate (see instructions on page 4); cool. In a medium saucepan combine the ¼ cup sugar and unflavored gelatin. Stir in milk. Cook and stir over low heat till gelatin dissolves. Gradually stir about *half* of the hot mixture into the egg yolks; return all to saucepan. Stir in the melted chocolate. Bring to boiling; reduce heat and boil gently for 2 minutes. Remove from heat. Stir in the cream of coconut and vanilla. Chill the gelatin mixture to the consistency of corn syrup, stirring occasionally. Remove from refrigerator (gelatin mixture will continue to set).

Immediately begin beating egg whites on medium speed of electric mixer till soft peaks form (tips curl over). Gradually add the 2 tablespoons sugar, beating on high speed till stiff peaks form (tips stand straight). When gelatin mixture is partially set (the consistency of unbeaten egg whites), fold in stiff-beaten egg whites. Beat the ½ cup whipping cream on medium speed of electric mixer till soft peaks form; fold into gelatin mixture. Turn into prepared soufflé dish; chill till firm. Before serving, remove the collar. Dollop unsweetened whipped cream atop soufflé. Sprinkle with toasted coconut. Makes 8 servings.

Chocolate Soufflé

Don't forget to try the chocolate mint and chocolate espresso variations—

2 squares (2 ounces)
   unsweetened chocolate
3 tablespoons butter *or*
   margarine
¼ cup all-purpose flour
¼ teaspoon salt
¾ cup milk
4 egg yolks
¼ cup sugar
2 tablespoons hot water
4 egg whites
½ teaspoon vanilla
¼ cup sugar
   Sifted powdered sugar
   Unsweetened whipped cream
      (optional)

For the collar, fold a 25-inch-long piece of foil lengthwise into thirds. Butter and sugar one side of the foil. Attach the foil, buttered and sugared side in, around the outside of an *ungreased* 1½-quart soufflé dish so that foil extends 1 inch above the dish. Secure the foil with tape. (Or, use an *ungreased* 2-quart soufflé dish without a foil collar.)

Melt unsweetened chocolate (see instructions on page 4); cool. In a small saucepan melt butter or margarine. Stir in flour and salt. Add milk; cook and stir till the mixture is thickened and bubbly. Cook and stir 1 minute more; remove from heat. In a large mixer bowl beat the egg yolks about 5 minutes or till thick and lemon colored. Gradually beat the hot thickened mixture into the beaten egg yolks. Stir together melted chocolate, ¼ cup sugar, and hot water; stir into the egg yolk mixture. Transfer to another bowl.

Wash the beaters and large mixer bowl thoroughly. In large mixer bowl beat the egg whites and vanilla on medium speed of electric mixer till soft peaks form (tips curl over). Gradually add ¼ cup sugar, beating on high speed of electric mixer till stiff peaks form (tips stand straight). Fold the chocolate mixture into the beaten egg whites. Turn mixture into the prepared soufflé dish. Bake in a 325° oven about 45 minutes or till a knife inserted near the center comes out clean. Quickly sprinkle sifted powdered sugar over the top of soufflé. Serve immediately with whipped cream, if desired. Makes 6 servings.

Chocolate Mint Soufflé: Prepare Chocolate Soufflé as directed above, *except* add 1 teaspoon *peppermint extract* to the egg whites and omit the vanilla.

Chocolate Espresso Soufflé: Prepare Chocolate Soufflé as directed above, *except* add 1 tablespoon powdered *instant espresso or* instant *coffee crystals* to the saucepan along with the milk.

How To Make the Collar for Chocolate Soufflé

For the collar, fold a 25-inch-long piece of foil lengthwise into thirds. Butter and sugar one side of the foil. Position the foil, buttered and sugared side in, around the outside of an *ungreased* 1½-quart soufflé dish so that the foil extends 1 inch above the dish; secure with tape.

CHOCOLATE

Ice Cream & Frozen Desserts

Brownie-Peanut Butter Ice Cream

You can use the Fudge Brownie recipe on page 28 for crumbled brownies—

2 cups sugar
2 cups light cream
2 cups whipping cream
6 well-beaten eggs
4 cups milk
1 tablespoon vanilla
2 cups crumbled brownies
1 cup chopped salted peanuts
1 cup peanut butter

In a heavy large saucepan combine the sugar, light cream, and whipping cream. Cook and stir over medium heat till the sugar dissolves. Stir about *half* of the hot mixture into the beaten eggs. Return all of the mixture to the saucepan. Cook and stir about 5 minutes more or till the mixture is slightly thickened and coats a metal spoon. Cool; stir in milk and vanilla. Cover and chill (chilling the mixture speeds freezing). Pour the mixture into a 5-quart ice cream freezer. Freeze according to manufacturer's directions. Remove the dasher; stir in the crumbled brownies, chopped peanuts, and peanut butter before ripening the ice cream. Makes about 3½ quarts.

Rich Chocolate Chip Ice Cream

A creamy, rich version of an ice cream favorite—

4 cups whipping cream
2 cups sugar
6 well-beaten eggs
4 cups milk
1 tablespoon vanilla
1½ cups semisweet chocolate pieces, chopped, *or* 1½ cups miniature semisweet chocolate pieces

In a heavy large saucepan combine the whipping cream and sugar. Cook and stir over medium heat till sugar dissolves. Stir about *half* of the hot mixture into the beaten eggs. Return all the mixture to the saucepan. Cook and stir about 5 minutes more or till the mixture is slightly thickened and coats a metal spoon. Cool; stir in milk and vanilla. Cover and chill (chilling the mixture speeds freezing). Stir in semisweet chocolate pieces; pour into a 5- or 6-quart ice cream freezer. Freeze according to manufacturer's directions. Makes about 4 quarts.

Mint-Chocolate Chip Ice Cream: Prepare Rich Chocolate Chip Ice Cream as directed above, *except* stir in ½ teaspoon *peppermint extract* and several drops *green food coloring* with the vanilla.

Homemade Ice Cream

The secret to making smooth homemade ice cream and other frozen desserts is to keep the ice crystals small. This is done by adding solids such as sugar, eggs, milk fat, and gelatin, which break up and separate the ice crystals. Air cells also keep the crystals small. Agitating the ice cream in an ice cream freezer incorporates air, which refines and smooths the texture. The same goal is achieved in refrigerator-frozen ice cream and frozen desserts by beating the partially frozen mixture and by folding in whipped cream or beaten egg whites.

Pictured opposite: Brownie-Peanut Butter Ice Cream

Pots de Crème Ice Cream

All you need is a small serving of this rich chocolate dessert—

½ cup water
1 6-ounce package (1 cup)
    semisweet chocolate
    pieces
3 egg yolks
1 4-ounce container frozen
    whipped dessert topping,
    thawed
  Fresh strawberries (optional)

In a small saucepan heat the water to boiling. Place the semisweet chocolate pieces in a blender container or a food processor bowl. Immediately pour the boiling water over the chocolate pieces. Cover and blend till the chocolate is melted. Add the egg yolks; cover and blend till the mixture is thickened and smooth. (If necessary, stop the blender or food processor and use a rubber spatula to scrape the sides of the container.) Transfer the chocolate mixture to a medium mixing bowl; fold the dessert topping into the chocolate mixture. Turn into a 9x5x3-inch loaf pan or an 8x8x2-inch baking pan. Cover and freeze several hours or till firm. Scoop or cut the ice cream into small squares to serve. Garnish each serving with a fresh strawberry, if desired. Makes 2½ cups.

Chocolate Irish Coffee Ice Cream

This ice cream makes an elegant finale to a special dinner—

4 beaten egg yolks
¾ cup sugar
¾ cup milk
¾ cup light cream
3 squares (3 ounces)
    semisweet chocolate,
    coarsely chopped
2 tablespoons instant coffee
    crystals
¼ cup Irish whiskey *or*
    bourbon whiskey
2 cups whipping cream

In a heavy medium saucepan combine the beaten egg yolks, sugar, milk, light cream, chopped chocolate, and coffee crystals. Cook and stir over medium heat till the mixture is slightly thickened and bubbly; remove from heat. (If mixture is flecked with chocolate, beat with rotary beater till smooth.) Place saucepan in a sink or bowl of ice water. Stir for 1 to 2 minutes or till cool. Stir in whiskey. In a large mixer bowl beat whipping cream on medium speed of electric mixer till soft peaks form. Fold in chocolate mixture. Turn into a 9x9x2-inch baking pan. Cover and freeze at least 6 hours or overnight till firm. Let stand at room temperature for 10 to 15 minutes before serving. Makes about 1½ quarts.

SHORT
SWEET

Chocolate and Amaretto Coffee Ice Cream

After chilling the bowl, you can prepare this in less than 10 minutes—

1 quart coffee ice cream
1 3- to 4-ounce bar milk
    chocolate, coarsely
    chopped, *or* ¾ cup milk
    chocolate pieces
¼ cup Amaretto

In a chilled medium mixing bowl stir the coffee ice cream just till softened. Stir in the milk chocolate and the Amaretto; cover and place in the freezer. Freeze several hours or overnight till firm. Makes about 1 quart.

Chocolate-Coated Ice Cream Cones

This is a fun treat that even adults will enjoy—

⅓ cup semisweet chocolate
    pieces
1 teaspoon shortening
6 sugar-type ice cream cones
1 tablespoon butter *or*
    margarine
1 tablespoon honey
⅛ teaspoon ground cinnamon
⅛ teaspoon ground nutmeg
1 cup crisp rice cereal,
    coarsely crushed
6 scoops cinnamon, coffee, *or*
    chocolate ice cream

Melt together the semisweet chocolate pieces and shortening (see instructions on page 4); cool slightly. Using a narrow metal spatula or a knife, carefully spread the melted chocolate mixture inside each ice cream cone. Set the chocolate-coated cones in the freezer for 5 to 10 minutes or till the chocolate hardens. (To set the cones upright, invert the lower portion of two empty egg cartons; insert the tips of the cones securely into the indentations down the middle of the inverted cartons. Place the cartons and cones in the freezer.)

Meanwhile, in a small saucepan combine the butter or margarine, honey, cinnamon, and nutmeg. Cook and stir over medium heat till the mixture is smooth; remove from heat. Add the crushed rice cereal, tossing gently to coat. Place 1 scoop of ice cream into each chocolate-coated ice cream cone. Carefully dip the top of each ice cream scoop into the rice cereal mixture to coat. Serve immediately or freeze for up to 6 hours. Makes 6 servings.

How To Make Chocolate-Coated Ice Cream Cones

To coat the insides of the ice cream cones, use a narrow metal spatula or a knife to carefully spread the melted chocolate mixture inside each sugar-type cone, as shown in the photo.

After coating the cones with the melted chocolate mixture, set them in the freezer for 5 to 10 minutes or till the chocolate hardens. To position the cones upright, invert the lower portion of two empty egg cartons. Insert the tips of the cones securely into the indentations down the middle of the inverted cartons, as shown in the photo. Place the cartons and the cones in the freezer.

Ice Cream Snowball Pie

This show-stopping dessert takes less than 30 minutes to prepare—

2 4-ounce bars German sweet cooking chocolate
3 tablespoons butter *or* margarine
2 cups crisp rice cereal
2 tablespoons butter *or* margarine
1 pint vanilla ice cream
1 pint mint-chocolate chip ice cream
1 pint strawberry ice cream

Set aside *2 ounces* (½ bar) of the German sweet cooking chocolate. To prepare the chocolate crust, melt together the remaining German sweet cooking chocolate and the 3 tablespoons butter or margarine (see instructions on page 4). In a medium mixing bowl combine the crisp rice cereal and the melted chocolate mixture; gently stir to coat. Using the back of a spoon, press the chocolate-cereal mixture onto the bottom and up the sides of a 9-inch pie plate. Place the chocolate crust in the freezer for 5 to 10 minutes or just till the chocolate in the crust is firm.

Meanwhile, melt together the reserved 2 ounces German sweet cooking chocolate and the 2 tablespoons butter or margarine (see instructions on page 4); cool slightly. Arrange scoops of vanilla, mint-chocolate chip, and strawberry ice cream in the chocolate crust. Pour the melted chocolate mixture over the ice cream scoops. Serve immediately. Makes 8 servings.

Peppermint Fudge Ribbon Pie

Chocolate ribbons run through this refreshing peppermint ice cream pie—

1½ cups finely crushed chocolate wafers (25 wafers)
⅓ cup butter *or* margarine, melted
1 5⅓-ounce can (⅔ cup) evaporated milk
2 squares (2 ounces) unsweetened chocolate, coarsely chopped
1 cup sugar
2 tablespoons butter *or* margarine
1 teaspoon vanilla
1 quart peppermint ice cream
1 cup whipping cream
¼ cup crushed peppermint candy (optional)

In a small mixing bowl stir together the crushed chocolate wafers and the ⅓ cup melted butter or margarine till well combined. Press the chocolate crumb mixture evenly onto the bottom and up the sides of a 9-inch pie plate. Chill the crust about 1 hour or till firm.

Meanwhile, for the chocolate sauce, in a medium saucepan combine evaporated milk and coarsely chopped unsweetened chocolate. Cook and stir over low heat till the chocolate is melted. Stir in sugar and the 2 tablespoons butter or margarine. Bring mixture to a gentle boil. Continue to cook over medium heat for 5 to 8 minutes or till the mixture is slightly thickened, stirring occasionally. Remove from heat. Stir in vanilla. Cool.

In a chilled medium mixing bowl stir the peppermint ice cream just till softened. Spread *half* of the softened ice cream in the prepared chocolate crust. Return the remaining ice cream to the freezer. Spread *half* of the chocolate sauce over the ice cream in the crust; freeze about 30 minutes or till firm. Let the remaining chocolate sauce stand at room temperature. Layer the remaining ice cream and chocolate sauce, ending with the chocolate sauce. (Soften ice cream to spread, if necessary.) Cover and freeze till firm.

Let the ice cream pie stand at room temperature about 10 minutes before serving. Meanwhile, in a small mixer bowl beat the whipping cream on medium speed of electric mixer just till stiff peaks form. Spoon the whipped cream over the top of the pie. Sprinkle with crushed peppermint candy, if desired. Serve the ice cream pie immediately. Makes 8 servings.

Pictured opposite: Ice Cream Snowball Pie

Hot Fudge-Rocky Road Sundaes

½ of a 6-ounce package (½ cup) semisweet chocolate pieces
2 tablespoons butter *or* margarine
½ cup tiny marshmallows
3 tablespoons rum *or* milk
¼ cup coarsely chopped pecans, toasted
Vanilla ice cream

In a heavy small saucepan combine semisweet chocolate pieces and butter or margarine. Cook and stir over low heat till melted. Add marshmallows and rum or milk. Cook and stir just till marshmallows begin to melt. Remove from heat; stir in the nuts. Place scoops of vanilla ice cream into 4 dessert dishes. Top with the warm chocolate-nut mixture. Makes enough topping for 4 servings.

Frozen Chocolate Yogurt Sandwiches

Try substituting graham crackers for the cookies next time you make this—

1 cup chocolate-flavored syrup
2 envelopes unflavored gelatin
1 7-ounce jar marshmallow creme
2 8-ounce cartons plain yogurt
1 cup milk
1 tablespoon vanilla
24 large *or* 48 small cookies (such as chocolate chip, sugar, *or* oatmeal-raisin)

In a small saucepan stir together chocolate-flavored syrup and gelatin; let stand 5 minutes. Cook and stir over low heat about 5 minutes or till gelatin is dissolved. Add marshmallow creme; stir till well combined. Remove from heat; cool slightly. Stir in yogurt, milk, and vanilla till well combined. Pour into a 13x9x2-inch baking pan; freeze several hours or till firm. Break frozen mixture into chunks; transfer to a large mixer bowl. Beat with an electric mixer till fluffy. Return to baking pan; freeze several hours or till firm.

To serve, cut frozen mixture into squares slightly smaller than cookies or cut into circles the same diameter as cookies. Sandwich each cutout between 2 cookies. Serve immediately or wrap and freeze for later use. Makes enough for 12 large or 24 small sandwiches.

Chocolate Peanut Butter 'n' Jelly Ice Cream Cups

3 squares (3 ounces) semisweet chocolate, coarsely chopped
¼ cup peanut butter
1¼ cups crisp rice cereal, coarsely crushed
¼ cup strawberry *or* grape jelly *or* orange marmalade
Ice cream
3 tablespoons chopped peanuts

In a heavy small saucepan combine the chocolate and peanut butter. Cook and stir over low heat till chocolate is melted. Remove from heat; stir in cereal. Butter four 6-ounce custard cups. Divide cereal mixture evenly among the cups. Press onto the bottoms and about halfway up the sides of the cups. Freeze for 5 to 10 minutes or till firm.

Before serving, dip bottom of custard cups in hot water for 5 to 10 seconds; carefully remove each chocolate shell. Spoon *1 tablespoon* of the jelly into the bottom of *each* shell. Fill with a scoop of ice cream. Sprinkle with peanuts. Serve immediately. Makes 4 servings.

Raspberry-Brownie Baked Alaska

1½ pints chocolate ice cream,
    slightly softened
1 pint vanilla ice cream,
    slightly softened
1 10-ounce package frozen
    red raspberries, thawed
½ cup butter *or* margarine
2 squares (2 ounces)
    unsweetened chocolate
1 cup sugar
2 eggs
1 teaspoon vanilla
¾ cup all-purpose flour
½ cup chopped walnuts
4 egg whites
1 teaspoon vanilla
¼ teaspoon cream of tartar
⅔ cup sugar

Line a chilled 1½-quart mixing bowl with clear plastic wrap. With the back of a large spoon, spread the chocolate ice cream in the mixing bowl to within ½ inch of the top of the bowl. Cover and freeze for 30 minutes. In a medium mixing bowl stir together the vanilla ice cream and *undrained* raspberries till well combined. Spoon the vanilla ice cream mixture into the center of the chocolate ice cream-lined mixing bowl. Cover and freeze about 5 hours or till the mixture is firm.

Meanwhile, grease and lightly flour an 8x1½-inch round baking pan. Melt together the butter or margarine and unsweetened chocolate (see instructions on page 4). In a large mixer bowl combine the 1 cup sugar and melted chocolate mixture. Add eggs and 1 teaspoon vanilla; beat on low speed of electric mixer just till combined (don't overbeat or brownie layer will rise too high, then fall). Stir in flour and chopped walnuts. Turn the batter into prepared pan. Bake in a 350° oven for 25 to 30 minutes or till a slight imprint remains after touching the surface lightly. Cool for 10 minutes on a wire rack. Remove from pan and cool thoroughly on a wire rack.

Place round brownie layer on a large sheet of foil. Invert the bowl of ice cream on top of the brownie layer; remove the clear plastic wrap. Bring the foil up around the brownie and ice cream to seal. Return to the freezer.

Thoroughly wash beaters and large mixer bowl. At serving time, in large mixer bowl beat egg whites, 1 teaspoon vanilla, and cream of tartar on medium speed of electric mixer till soft peaks form. Gradually add the ⅔ cup sugar, beating on high speed of electric mixer till stiff peaks form. Unwrap the ice cream-topped brownie; transfer to an ungreased baking sheet, brownie side down. Spread with the egg white mixture, sealing to the edges of the brownie and baking sheet all around. Swirl to make peaks. Place oven rack in lowest position. Bake in a 500° oven about 3 minutes or till golden. Slice and serve immediately. Makes 16 servings.

How To Layer Raspberry-Brownie Baked Alaska

With the back of a large spoon, spread chocolate ice cream in the chilled bowl, spreading to within ½ inch of the top of bowl. Spoon the vanilla ice cream mixture into the center of the chocolate ice cream-lined bowl, as shown in the photo.

CHOCOLATE

Puddings
Custards & More

Mocha Mousse

You can use instant espresso to boost the coffee flavor in this rich dessert—

2 tablespoons boiling water
1 teaspoon dry instant espresso *or* instant coffee crystals
¼ cup sugar
2 squares (2 ounces) semisweet chocolate, coarsely chopped
2 slightly beaten egg yolks
½ teaspoon vanilla
2 egg whites
⅛ teaspoon cream of tartar
2 tablespoons sugar
½ cup whipping cream
Unsweetened whipped cream (optional)
Chocolate Curls (see instructions, page 90)

In a heavy large saucepan combine the boiling water and instant espresso or coffee crystals. Add the ¼ cup sugar; cook and stir over medium heat till sugar is dissolved. Add the chopped chocolate; stir till melted. Remove the saucepan from heat.

Gradually stir the hot mixture into the beaten egg yolks; return all to saucepan. Cook and stir over medium heat till slightly thickened and bubbly; reduce heat. Cook and stir for 2 minutes more. Remove from heat; stir in vanilla. Cool slightly, stirring occasionally.

In a small mixer bowl beat egg whites and cream of tartar till soft peaks form. Gradually add the 2 tablespoons sugar, beating till stiff peaks form. Fold the beaten egg whites into the chocolate mixture.

Beat the ½ cup whipping cream till soft peaks form. Fold the whipped cream into the chocolate mixture. Spoon into 3 or 4 individual dessert dishes or into a serving bowl. Cover and chill in the refrigerator about 3 hours or till firm. If desired, dollop each serving with additional unsweetened whipped cream. Garnish with Chocolate Curls. Makes 3 or 4 servings.

Vanilla Crème with Sherry-Raspberry Sauce

You'll enjoy this light, fluffy dessert made with confectioner's coating—

3 ounces vanilla-flavored confectioner's coating, coarsely chopped
¼ cup whipping cream
2 slightly beaten egg yolks
¼ cup butter *or* margarine
½ teaspoon vanilla
2 egg whites
⅛ teaspoon cream of tartar
½ cup whipping cream
Sherry-Raspberry Sauce

In a saucepan combine confectioner's coating and the ¼ cup whipping cream. Cook and stir over medium heat till confectioner's coating is melted. Gradually stir about *half* of the hot mixture into the beaten egg yolks; return all to saucepan. Cook and stir over medium heat till slightly thickened and bubbly; reduce heat. Cook and stir for 2 minutes more. Remove from heat; stir in butter or margarine and vanilla. Cool slightly, stirring occasionally.

In a small mixer bowl beat egg whites and cream of tartar till stiff peaks form. Fold into the egg yolk mixture. Beat the ½ cup whipping cream till soft peaks form. Fold into the egg white mixture. Spoon into 4 to 6 individual dessert dishes or into a serving bowl. Cover and chill about 2 hours or till firm. To serve, prepare Sherry-Raspberry Sauce; spoon atop chilled dessert. Makes 4 to 6 servings.

Sherry-Raspberry Sauce: Thaw one 10-ounce package frozen *red raspberries*. Drain raspberries, reserving ½ cup syrup; set aside. In a 1-quart saucepan combine 2 tablespoons *sugar* and 1 tablespoon *cornstarch*. Stir in the reserved raspberry syrup and ⅓ cup *cream sherry*. Cook and stir till thickened and bubbly. Cook and stir for 2 minutes more. Stir in the drained raspberries. Cool slightly.

Pictured opposite: Mocha Mousse
Chocolate Curls (see page 90)

Chocolate Pudding

Try this creamy chocolate pudding and two just-as-yummy variations—

¾ cup sugar
2 tablespoons cornstarch
¼ teaspoon salt
2 cups milk
2 squares (2 ounces)
    unsweetened chocolate,
    coarsely chopped
2 slightly beaten egg yolks
    or 1 beaten egg
2 tablespoons butter *or*
    margarine
1½ teaspoons vanilla

In a heavy medium saucepan combine the sugar, cornstarch, and salt. Stir in the milk and coarsely chopped chocolate. Cook and stir over medium heat till the mixture is thickened and bubbly. Cook and stir for 2 minutes more. Remove the saucepan from heat.

Gradually stir about *1 cup* of the hot mixture into the beaten egg yolks or whole egg. Return the egg mixture to the chocolate mixture in the saucepan. Cook and stir over low heat for 1 to 2 minutes more; *do not boil.* Remove the saucepan from heat. Add the butter or margarine and vanilla; stir till the butter is melted.

Pour the pudding into a 1-quart bowl. Cover the surface with clear plastic wrap. Chill in the refrigerator, without stirring, about 3 hours or till cold. To serve, spoon the pudding into individual dessert dishes. Makes 4 servings.

Chocolate-Mint Pudding: Prepare Chocolate Pudding as above, *except* reduce the vanilla to 1 teaspoon and stir in ¼ teaspoon *peppermint extract* with the butter or margarine and vanilla. Before serving, sprinkle crushed *hard peppermint candy* atop each serving, if desired.

Almond-Mocha Pudding: Prepare Chocolate Pudding as above, *except* add 1 tablespoon instant *coffee crystals* to the sugar, cornstarch, and salt. Reduce the vanilla to 1 teaspoon and stir in ½ cup toasted, chopped *almonds* and ¼ teaspoon *almond extract* with the butter or margarine and vanilla. Before serving, sprinkle additional toasted, chopped *almonds* atop each serving, if desired.

Steamed Fudge Pudding

This nutty dessert is a cross between a pudding and a cake—

1 6-ounce package (1 cup)
    semisweet chocolate
    pieces
4 slightly beaten eggs
2 cups milk
½ cup packed brown sugar
¾ teaspoon ground cinnamon
¼ teaspoon salt
4 cups dry bread cubes
½ cup chopped nuts
    Whipped cream (optional)

Melt the semisweet chocolate pieces (see instructions on page 4). In a large mixing bowl combine the slightly beaten eggs, milk, brown sugar, cinnamon, salt, and the melted semisweet chocolate. Stir in the dry bread cubes and chopped nuts. Turn the chocolate mixture into an ungreased 10x6x2-inch baking dish.

Place the filled baking dish into a 13x9x2-inch baking pan set on an oven rack. Pour boiling water into the large pan around the smaller dish to a depth of 1 inch, being careful not to spill any water into the chocolate mixture. Bake, uncovered, in a 350° oven for 60 to 65 minutes or till a knife inserted near the center of the pudding comes out clean. Serve the pudding warm. Cut into squares to serve. If desired, spoon some whipped cream atop each serving. Makes 8 servings.

Flaming Orange-Chocolate Crepes

Orange-filled chocolate crepes poach in a mellow orange liqueur sauce—

1 slightly beaten egg
¾ cup milk
½ cup all-purpose flour
2 tablespoons sugar
2 tablespoons Dutch process cocoa powder *or* unsweetened cocoa powder
2 teaspoons cooking oil
1 3-ounce package cream cheese, softened
2 tablespoons powdered sugar
1 teaspoon orange liqueur
2 tablespoons sugar
1½ teaspoons cornstarch
⅓ cup orange juice
¼ cup orange liqueur
1 tablespoon butter *or* margarine
2 tablespoons brandy

For crepes, in a mixing bowl combine the egg, milk, flour, 2 tablespoons sugar, cocoa powder, and cooking oil; beat with a rotary beater till well combined. Heat a lightly greased 6-inch skillet; remove from heat. Spoon in *2 tablespoons* of the batter; lift and tilt skillet to spread batter. Return to heat; brown on one side *only*. (*Or,* cook the batter on an inverted crepe pan.) Invert the skillet or crepe pan over paper toweling; remove crepe. Repeat with remaining batter to make 8 crepes, greasing the skillet occasionally. Set the crepes aside.

For the filling, in a mixing bowl combine the softened cream cheese, powdered sugar, and the 1 teaspoon orange liqueur; stir till smooth. Gently spread about *2 teaspoons* of the cream cheese filling over the unbrowned side of *each* crepe, leaving a ¼-inch rim around edge. Roll up the crepes jelly-roll style; set aside.

For the sauce, in a 10-inch skillet or chafing dish combine 2 tablespoons sugar and cornstarch. Stir in the orange juice, the ¼ cup orange liqueur, and butter or margarine. Cook and stir over medium heat till the mixture is thickened and bubbly. Arrange the filled crepes, seam side down, in the warm sauce in the skillet. Cook, uncovered, about 2 minutes more or till the crepes are heated through, constantly spooning the sauce over the crepes during heating.

To flame, pour the brandy into a ladle; warm over a burner till brandy almost simmers. *Do not boil.* Quickly ignite and pour the flaming brandy over crepes and sauce. Wait till the flame subsides to serve. Spoon some of the warm sauce over each serving. Makes 4 servings.

How To Flame Orange-Chocolate Crepes

Pour brandy into a ladle; warm over a burner till brandy almost simmers. *Do not boil.* Quickly ignite the brandy with a long match. Pour the flaming brandy over the crepes and sauce in the skillet or chafing dish, as shown in the photo.

Chocolate Stirred Custard

Make sure the chocolate is completely melted for a velvety smooth custard—

2 cups milk
½ cup sugar
2 squares (2 ounces)
    unsweetened chocolate,
    coarsely chopped
3 slightly beaten eggs
1 teaspoon vanilla

In a heavy medium saucepan combine the milk, sugar, and coarsely chopped chocolate. Cook and stir over medium heat till the mixture is bubbly and the chocolate is melted. Remove the saucepan from heat. (If flecks of chocolate remain, beat the hot mixture with a rotary beater or a wire whisk till smooth.)

Gradually stir about *1 cup* of the hot mixture into the beaten eggs. Return the egg mixture to the chocolate mixture in the saucepan. Cook and stir over low heat for 1 to 2 minutes more or till mixture coats a metal spoon; *do not boil.* Remove from heat. Stir in the vanilla.

Immediately cool the mixture by transferring it to a 1-quart bowl and placing the bowl in a sink or larger bowl of ice water. Stir for 1 to 2 minutes. Cover the surface with clear plastic wrap. Chill in the refrigerator, without stirring, about 3 hours or till set. To serve, spoon the custard into individual dessert dishes. Makes 6 servings.

Chocolate Pots de Crème

This classic French dessert is traditionally served in small cups—

1 cup light cream
1 4-ounce package German
    sweet cooking chocolate,
    coarsely chopped
1 tablespoon sugar
3 slightly beaten egg yolks
½ teaspoon vanilla
    Whipped cream (optional)

In a heavy small saucepan combine the light cream, coarsely chopped chocolate, and sugar. Cook and stir over medium-low heat till the chocolate is melted and the mixture is smooth and slightly thickened. Remove the saucepan from heat.

Gradually stir about *half* of the hot mixture into the beaten egg yolks; return the egg yolk mixture to the chocolate mixture in the saucepan. Cook and stir over medium-low heat for 2 to 3 minutes more. Remove the saucepan from heat. Stir in the vanilla.

Pour the chocolate mixture into 4 to 6 pots de crème or demitasse cups or small sherbet dishes. Cover and chill in the refrigerator several hours or till firm. Before serving, garnish each serving with whipped cream, if desired. Makes 4 to 6 servings.

Cooling Custards and Puddings

To cool hot stirred custard or pudding, transfer it from the warm saucepan to a bowl. Keep a "skin" from forming on the top of the thickened mixture by carefully placing a piece of clear plastic wrap or waxed paper directly onto the surface. Chill in the refrigerator, without stirring, for several hours or till the custard or pudding is cold.

Before serving, gently peel the plastic wrap or waxed paper from the surface and discard. To serve, spoon the custard or pudding into individual dessert dishes.

Chocolate-Nutmeg Bavarian

¼ cup sugar
1 envelope unflavored gelatin
¼ teaspoon ground nutmeg
1 cup light cream *or* milk
6 squares (6 ounces) semisweet chocolate, coarsely chopped, *or* one 6-ounce package (1 cup) semisweet chocolate pieces
2 slightly beaten egg yolks
2 egg whites
1 teaspoon vanilla
⅛ teaspoon cream of tartar
¼ cup sugar
1 cup whipping cream
Whipped cream (optional)
Fresh fruit* (optional)

In heavy medium saucepan combine ¼ cup sugar, gelatin, and nutmeg. Stir in light cream or milk and chocolate. Cook and stir over low heat till gelatin is dissolved and chocolate is melted. Remove from heat.

Gradually stir about *half* of the hot mixture into the beaten egg yolks; return all to saucepan. Cook and stir over medium heat till slightly thickened and bubbly; reduce heat. Cook and stir for 2 minutes more. Remove from heat. Cover and chill in the refrigerator till the mixture is the consistency of corn syrup. Remove from the refrigerator (gelatin mixture will continue to set).

Immediately combine egg whites, vanilla, and cream of tartar in a small mixer bowl; beat on medium speed of electric mixer till soft peaks form (tips curl over). Gradually add ¼ cup sugar, beating till stiff peaks form (tips stand straight). When the gelatin mixture is the consistency of unbeaten egg whites (partially set), fold in the stiff-beaten egg whites.

Beat the whipping cream till soft peaks form; fold into the gelatin mixture. Chill till the mixture mounds when spooned. Turn into a 5- or 6-cup ring mold. Cover and chill in the refrigerator about 6 hours or till firm. Before serving, unmold onto a serving plate. If desired, pipe additional whipped cream around the bottom outside edge and fill the center of the dessert with fresh fruit. Makes 12 servings.

Note: For fresh fruit, you can use sliced *strawberries or bananas, orange sections, raspberries, or* halved *cherries.*

Fluffy Mint-Chocolate Cups

Pure chocolate cups cradle a luscious mint-chocolate filling—

6 squares (6 ounces) semisweet chocolate, coarsely chopped
1 tablespoon shortening
1 package 4-serving-size *regular* chocolate pudding mix
1½ cups milk
4 cream-filled chocolate-covered peppermint patties, cut up (¼ cup)
1 cup whipping cream
2 cream-filled chocolate-covered peppermint patties, cut up (2 tablespoons)

For chocolate cups, melt together semisweet chocolate and shortening (see instructions on page 4). Using a clean, small paintbrush, brush the melted chocolate onto the bottom and up the side of each paper cup till about ⅛ inch thick. Wipe off any chocolate that may have run over the top. Chill the chocolate cups in the refrigerator about 30 minutes or till hardened.

Meanwhile, for the filling, in a heavy medium saucepan combine the pudding mix, milk, and the 4 cut-up peppermint patties. Cook and stir over medium heat till thickened and bubbly. Cook and stir for 2 minutes more. Remove the saucepan from heat. Cover the surface with clear plastic wrap; cool slightly.

Carefully peel the paper cups away from the hardened chocolate cups. Stir the cooled pudding mixture. In a mixer bowl beat the whipping cream till soft peaks form; fold into the pudding mixture. Fill *each* chocolate cup with about ¼ *cup* of the pudding mixture. Cover and chill the filled chocolate cups in the refrigerator about 2 hours or till cold. Before serving, sprinkle the filled cups with the 2 cut-up peppermint patties. Makes 12 servings.

Tropical Chocolate Parfaits

Create this chocolate, pineapple, and coconut dessert in about 15 minutes—

1 17½-ounce can chocolate
    pudding
½ of a 6-ounce package (½ cup)
    miniature semisweet
    chocolate pieces
½ cup dairy sour cream
1 20-ounce can crushed
    pineapple, drained
½ cup coconut

In a mixing bowl stir together the chocolate pudding, chocolate pieces, and sour cream. Combine the crushed pineapple and coconut. In 6 parfait glasses alternately layer pudding mixture and pineapple mixture, starting with the pudding mixture. Cover and chill in the refrigerator till serving time. Makes 6 servings.

Layered Chocolate Terrine

4 squares (4 ounces)
    semisweet chocolate
18 ladyfingers, split, *or* 1 frozen
    loaf pound cake, thawed
½ cup butter *or* margarine
1 cup sifted powdered sugar
1 tablespoon crème de cacao
    (optional)
1 egg
½ cup whipping cream
½ cup toasted, chopped
    almonds *or* chopped
    pistachio nuts
    Raspberry Sauce

Melt the chocolate (see instructions on page 4); cool. Line an 8x4x2-inch loaf pan with clear plastic wrap. Arrange *6* of the ladyfinger halves crosswise, side by side, in the bottom of the pan, trimming if necessary to fit. Line *each* long side of pan with *6* ladyfinger halves; trim, if necessary. (*Or,* cut the thawed pound cake horizontally into 6 layers. Place *1* of the layers in the bottom of the loaf pan, trimming if necessary to fit. Line *each* long side of pan with *1* layer.) Trim even with the top of the pan.

For the filling, in a large mixer bowl beat butter or margarine on medium speed of electric mixer for 30 seconds. Gradually add the powdered sugar, beating till light and fluffy. Add the melted chocolate and crème de cacao, if desired; beat till combined. Add the egg; beat till smooth. In a small mixer bowl beat the whipping cream till soft peaks form; fold into the chocolate mixture. Fold in the chopped almonds or pistachio nuts.

To assemble terrine, spread *1 cup* of the chocolate filling over the bottom ladyfinger or cake layer in the loaf pan. Top with *6* more ladyfinger halves or *1* cake layer, trimming if necessary. Spread another *1 cup* filling atop; top with another ladyfinger or cake layer. Spread with remaining chocolate filling, and top with a ladyfinger or cake layer. Cover and chill terrine about 3 hours or till cold. Prepare Raspberry Sauce; cover and chill.

To serve, unmold the terrine onto a serving platter. Remove plastic wrap. Spoon some of the Raspberry Sauce atop. Cut terrine crosswise into slices. Pass the remaining Raspberry Sauce. Makes 12 servings.

Raspberry Sauce: Measure 2 cups fresh *or* frozen *red raspberries.* In a small saucepan crush ½ *cup* of the raspberries. Add ⅔ cup *water.* Bring to boiling; reduce heat. Simmer, uncovered, for 2 minutes; sieve. Combine ⅓ cup *sugar* and 1 tablespoon *cornstarch;* stir into sieved mixture. Return to saucepan. Cook and stir till thickened and bubbly. Cook and stir for 2 minutes more. Remove from heat. Stir in ¼ teaspoon *vanilla.* Stir remaining raspberries into sauce.

Pictured opposite: Layered Chocolate Terrine

Velvety Hot Fudge Sauce

You can reheat this scrumptious sauce later for additional servings—

3 squares (3 ounces)
    semisweet chocolate
¼ cup butter *or* margarine
1 5⅓-ounce can (⅔ cup)
    evaporated milk
½ cup sugar
1 teaspoon vanilla

In a heavy medium saucepan melt chocolate and butter or margarine over low heat, stirring constantly. Stir in evaporated milk and sugar. Cook and stir over medium heat till sugar is dissolved and mixture is slightly thickened and bubbly. Remove from heat. Add vanilla; stir till smooth.

To serve, spoon the warm sauce over ice cream, fresh fruit, or pound cake, if desired. Store any leftover sauce, covered, in the refrigerator. To reheat, cook and stir over low heat till heated through. Makes about 1⅓ cups sauce.

Chocolate-Drizzled Pears with Rum Sauce

These elegant pears float on a cloud of whipped cream—

⅓ cup semisweet chocolate
    pieces
2 teaspoons shortening
1 16-ounce can pear halves
1 tablespoon brown sugar
1 teaspoon cornstarch
1 teaspoon lemon juice
1 tablespoon rum
1 cup whipping cream

Melt together semisweet chocolate pieces and shortening (see instructions on page 4). Drain the pear halves, reserving ½ cup of the syrup. Pat the pear halves dry with paper toweling. Place the pear halves, flat side down, on a wire rack set over waxed paper. Using a spoon, drizzle the chocolate mixture over pear halves. Chill in the refrigerator about 30 minutes or till the chocolate is hardened.

Meanwhile, for the sauce, in a small saucepan combine the brown sugar and cornstarch. Stir in the ½ cup reserved pear syrup and the lemon juice. Cook and stir over medium heat till the mixture is thickened and bubbly. Cook and stir for 2 minutes more. Remove from heat; cool slightly. Stir in the rum. Chill, if desired.

Before serving, in a small mixer bowl beat the whipping cream till soft peaks form. Spread the whipped cream onto a small serving platter or onto 6 individual dessert plates, building up the edges slightly. Arrange the chocolate-drizzled pears atop the whipped cream. Pass the sauce. Makes 6 servings.

How To Make Chocolate-Drizzled Pears

Place the well-drained pear halves, flat side down, on a wire rack set over waxed paper. Using a spoon, drizzle the chocolate mixture over the pear halves, as shown in the photo. Chill in the refrigerator to harden the chocolate.

Chocolate Fondue

This fondue, as well as its three variations, can pinch-hit as a sauce—

8 squares (8 ounces)
  semisweet chocolate,
  coarsely chopped
1 14-ounce can (1¼ cups)
  Eagle Brand sweetened
  condensed milk
⅓ cup milk
  Assorted fondue dippers*

In a heavy medium saucepan melt the chocolate over low heat, stirring constantly. Stir in the sweetened condensed milk and regular milk; heat through. Transfer to a fondue pot; place over a fondue burner.

Spear desired fondue dipper with a fondue fork; dip into the warm chocolate fondue, swirling to coat with the mixture. (The swirling is important to keep the mixture in motion so it doesn't set up.) If the fondue mixture thickens while standing, stir in some additional regular milk. Makes 8 servings.

Mocha Fondue: Prepare the Chocolate Fondue as directed above, *except* substitute ⅓ cup *strong coffee* for the regular milk.

Caramel-Chocolate Fondue: Prepare the Chocolate Fondue as directed above, *except* substitute one 12-ounce jar *caramel topping* for the regular milk.

Chocolate and Peanut Butter Fondue: Prepare the Chocolate Fondue as directed above, *except* stir in ⅓ cup *creamy peanut butter* with the sweetened condensed milk and the regular milk.

*Note: For fondue dippers, use *angel cake or pound cake squares, marshmallows, whole strawberries, banana slices, or pineapple chunks.*

Chocolate-Caramel Popcorn

Indulge in this chocolate spin-off of traditional caramel corn—

8 cups popped popcorn
1 cup dry roasted peanuts
¼ cup sunflower nuts
  (optional)
¾ cup packed brown sugar
⅓ cup butter *or* margarine
3 tablespoons light corn syrup
2 tablespoons milk
½ of a 6-ounce package (½ cup)
  milk chocolate pieces *or*
  semisweet chocolate
  pieces
¼ teaspoon baking soda
¼ teaspoon vanilla

Remove and discard all the unpopped kernels from popped corn. In a 17x12x2-inch baking pan combine the popcorn, peanuts, and sunflower nuts, if desired; set aside.

In a heavy 1½-quart saucepan combine the brown sugar, butter or margarine, corn syrup, and milk. Cook and stir over medium heat till the butter is melted and the mixture is boiling. Cook, without stirring, for 5 minutes more. Remove from heat. Add the chocolate pieces; stir till melted. Stir in the baking soda and vanilla.

Pour the chocolate mixture over the popcorn mixture; stir to coat evenly. Bake, uncovered, in a 300° oven for 15 minutes; stir once. Bake for 5 to 10 minutes more or till mixture is crisp; cool to room temperature. Transfer to a large bowl to serve. Store any leftover mixture in an airtight container. Makes 9 cups.

CHOCOLATE

Breads

Chocolate-Caramel Pecan Rolls

You'll find creamy chocolate inside the rolls, as well as drizzled on top—

4¼ to 4¾ cups all-purpose flour
1 package active dry yeast
1 cup milk
⅓ cup sugar
⅓ cup butter *or* margarine
½ teaspoon salt
2 eggs
⅓ cup semisweet chocolate
    pieces
3 tablespoons butter *or*
    margarine
  Caramel Sauce
½ cup chopped pecans
⅔ cup semisweet chocolate
    pieces
2 tablespoons butter *or*
    margarine

In a large mixer bowl combine *2 cups* of the flour and the yeast. Heat milk, sugar, the ⅓ cup butter or margarine, and salt just till warm (115° to 120°) and butter is almost melted; stir constantly. Add to flour mixture; add eggs. Beat on low speed of electric mixer for ½ minute, scraping sides of bowl constantly. Beat 3 minutes on high speed. Using a spoon, stir in as much of the remaining flour as you can. Turn out onto a lightly floured surface. Knead in enough of the remaining flour to make a moderately stiff dough that is smooth and elastic (6 to 8 minutes total). Place in a lightly greased bowl; turn once to grease surface. Cover; let rise in a warm place till double (about 1 hour). Punch down; divide dough in half. Cover; let rest 10 minutes.

Meanwhile, melt together ⅓ cup chocolate pieces and the 3 tablespoons butter (see instructions on page 4); cool. Roll half of the dough into a 12x8-inch rectangle. Brush half of the melted chocolate mixture over dough. Roll up jelly-roll style, beginning from a long side; moisten edge with water and pinch to seal seam well. Slice into 12 pieces. Repeat with remaining dough. Prepare Caramel Sauce. Divide sauce evenly between two 9x1½-inch round baking pans. Sprinkle with nuts. Place rolls in prepared pans. Cover; let rise till nearly double (about 30 minutes). Bake in a 375° oven for 20 to 25 minutes or till golden brown. Invert onto a serving plate or a wire rack. Melt together the ⅔ cup chocolate pieces and 2 tablespoons butter. Drizzle over warm rolls. Makes 24 rolls.

Caramel Sauce: In a small saucepan combine ⅔ cup packed *brown sugar*, ¼ cup *butter or margarine*, and 2 tablespoons *light corn syrup*. Cook and stir over medium heat till butter is melted.

Yeast Bread Tips

Making yeast bread doesn't require a magic touch, but the tips that follow can help ensure a perfect product every time.

When kneading dough, here's a good way to recognize the various stages specified in recipes. *Soft dough* is too sticky to knead and often is used for batter breads. *Moderately soft dough* is slightly sticky, kneads easily on a lightly floured surface, and is used for most of the yeast breads in this chapter. *Moderately stiff dough* is somewhat firm to the touch and kneads easily on a lightly floured surface. *Stiff dough* is firm to the touch and is easily rolled on a lightly floured surface.

When the recipe gives a range on the amount of flour, start by adding the smaller amount. Remember that the flour used in kneading the dough also is part of this measured amount.

When you make bread on humid days, the dough may require more flour than the amount stated in the recipe.

Pictured opposite: Chocolate-Caramel Pecan Rolls

Chocolate Bismarcks

This versatile recipe also can be used to make yeast doughnuts—

2 packages active dry yeast
⅓ cup warm water (110°
   to 115°)
3 to 3½ cups all-purpose flour
⅓ cup sugar
⅓ cup milk
¼ cup shortening
2 squares (2 ounces)
   semisweet chocolate,
   coarsely chopped
½ teaspoon salt
2 eggs
   Shortening *or* cooking oil for
   deep-fat frying
   Creamy Chocolate Filling
   Sifted powdered sugar

Dissolve yeast in warm water. In a large mixer bowl place *1½ cups* of the flour. In a saucepan heat the sugar, milk, shortening, chocolate, and salt over low heat till chocolate is melted; stir constantly. If necessary, cool just till warm (115° to 120°). Add to flour in mixer bowl; add eggs and yeast mixture. Beat on low speed of electric mixer for ½ minute, scraping sides of bowl constantly. Beat 3 minutes on high speed. Using a spoon, stir in as much of the remaining flour as you can. Turn out onto a lightly floured surface. Knead in enough of the remaining flour to make a moderately soft dough that is smooth and elastic (3 to 5 minutes total). Shape into a ball. Place in a lightly greased bowl; turn once to grease surface. Cover; let rise in a warm place till double (about 1 hour).

Punch down; divide dough in half. Cover; let rest 10 minutes. Roll each half of dough to ½-inch thickness. Cut with a floured 2½-inch biscuit cutter, pressing straight down. Reroll and cut trimmings. Cover; let rise in warm place till *very light* (30 to 45 minutes). Heat shortening or oil for deep-fat frying to 375°. Fry 2 or 3 rounds of dough at a time about 2 minutes or till golden brown, turning once. Drain on paper toweling. With a sharp knife, carefully cut a wide slit in the side of each bismarck. Spoon 2 teaspoons of the Chocolate Filling into each bismarck. (*Or*, fit a decorating bag with a writing tube; fill bag with Chocolate Filling. Insert tube into slit in each bismarck; squeeze in about 2 teaspoons filling.) Roll bismarcks in powdered sugar. Makes 20 to 24 bismarcks.

Creamy Chocolate Filling: In a small saucepan combine ½ cup *sugar* and 2 tablespoons all-purpose *flour*. Stir in 1 cup *milk* and 1 square (1 ounce) *semisweet chocolate,* coarsely chopped. Cook and stir over medium heat till thickened and bubbly. Cook and stir about 1 minute more. Gradually stir about *half* of the hot mixture into 1 beaten *egg;* return all of the mixture to saucepan. Cook and stir just till bubbly. Remove from heat. Stir in 1 tablespoon *butter or margarine* and 1 teaspoon *vanilla.* Cover surface with clear plastic wrap. Cool without stirring.

How To Fill Chocolate Bismarcks

Cut a slit in the side of each bismarck. Spoon 2 teaspoons chocolate filling into each bismarck, as shown in photo. *Or,* fit a decorating bag with a writing tube; fill bag with filling. Insert tube into slit in each bismarck; squeeze in about 2 teaspoons filling.

Choco-Peanut Butter Ring

Chocolate and peanut butter lovers are crazy about this one—

2 to 2½ cups all-purpose flour
1 package active dry yeast
½ cup milk
¼ cup sugar
2 tablespoons butter *or* margarine
¼ teaspoon salt
1 egg
½ of a 6-ounce package (½ cup) semisweet chocolate pieces
¼ cup sugar
¼ cup peanut butter
2 tablespoons butter *or* margarine

In a large mixer bowl combine *1 cup* of the flour and the yeast. Heat milk, ¼ cup sugar, 2 tablespoons butter, and salt just till warm (115° to 120°) and butter is almost melted; stir constantly. Add to flour mixture. Add egg. Beat on low speed of electric mixer for ½ minute, scraping sides of bowl constantly. Beat 3 minutes on high speed. Using a spoon, stir in as much remaining flour as you can. Turn out onto a lightly floured surface. Knead in enough remaining flour to make a moderately soft dough that is smooth and elastic (3 to 5 minutes total). Shape into a ball. Place in a greased bowl; turn once to grease surface. Cover; let rise in a warm place till double (about 1¼ hours). Punch down dough. Cover; let rest 10 minutes.

Meanwhile, melt chocolate (see instructions on page 4); cool. Beat together ¼ cup sugar, peanut butter, and 2 tablespoons butter or margarine till smooth. Stir in melted chocolate. Roll dough into a 22x9-inch rectangle. Spread chocolate mixture over dough to within ½ inch of the edges. Roll up jelly-roll style, beginning from a long side; moisten edge with water and pinch to seal. Place on a greased baking sheet; seal ends together to form a ring. Cover; let rise till nearly double (35 to 45 minutes). Bake in a 350° oven for 25 to 30 minutes or till golden brown, covering with foil the last 10 to 15 minutes to prevent overbrowning. Cool on a wire rack. Makes 1 ring.

Chocolate Swirl Coffee Cake

4 to 4½ cups all-purpose flour
2 packages active dry yeast
¾ cup sugar
⅔ cup water
½ cup butter *or* margarine
⅓ cup evaporated milk
½ teaspoon salt
4 egg yolks
¾ cup semisweet chocolate pieces
⅓ cup evaporated milk
2 tablespoons sugar
½ teaspoon ground cinnamon
¼ cup all-purpose flour
¼ cup sugar
1 teaspoon ground cinnamon
¼ cup butter *or* margarine
¼ cup chopped nuts

Using the 4 to 4½ cups flour, in a large mixer bowl combine *1½ cups* flour and the yeast. Heat ¾ cup sugar, water, ½ cup butter, ⅓ cup evaporated milk, and salt just till warm (115° to 120°) and butter is almost melted; stir constantly. Add to flour mixture. Add egg yolks. Beat on low speed of electric mixer for ½ minute, scraping bowl. Beat 3 minutes on high speed. Using a spoon, stir in as much remaining flour as you can. Knead in enough remaining flour to make a moderately soft dough that is smooth and elastic (3 to 5 minutes total). Place in a greased bowl; turn once. Cover; let rise in a warm place till double (about 2 hours). Punch down. Cover; let rest 10 minutes.

Heat chocolate, ⅓ cup evaporated milk, 2 tablespoons sugar, and ½ teaspoon cinnamon over low heat till chocolate is melted; cool. Roll dough into an 18x10-inch rectangle. Spread with chocolate mixture. Roll up jelly-roll style, beginning from long side; seal seam. Seal ends to form a ring. Place in a greased 10-inch tube pan. Combine ¼ cup flour, ¼ cup sugar, and 1 teaspoon cinnamon. Cut in ¼ cup butter; stir in nuts. Sprinkle over dough. Cover; let rise till nearly double (about 1¼ hours). Bake on lower rack in a 350° oven for 45 to 50 minutes or till brown. Cool 15 minutes; remove from pan. Makes 1 coffee cake.

Chocolate Pecan Braid

Braiding the dough is an easy way to give bread a different look—

2½ to 3 cups all-purpose flour
⅓ cup unsweetened cocoa powder
1 package active dry yeast
¾ cup milk
½ cup sugar
¼ cup butter *or* margarine
½ teaspoon salt
1 egg
½ cup finely chopped pecans
  Confectioner's Icing
  Pecan halves (optional)
  Maraschino cherries (optional)

In a large mixer bowl combine ¾ *cup* of the flour, the cocoa powder, and yeast. Heat milk, sugar, butter or margarine, and salt just till warm (115° to 120°) and butter is almost melted; stir constantly. Add to flour mixture; add egg. Beat on low speed of electric mixer for ½ minute, scraping sides of bowl constantly. Beat 3 minutes on high speed. Stir in the finely chopped pecans. Using a spoon, stir in as much of the remaining flour as you can. Turn out onto a lightly floured surface. Knead in enough of the remaining flour to make a moderately soft dough that is smooth and elastic (3 to 5 minutes total). Shape into a ball. Place in a lightly greased bowl; turn once to grease surface. Cover; let rise in a warm place till double (about 1½ hours).

Punch down; divide dough into thirds. Cover; let rest 10 minutes. Roll each third into a 16-inch-long rope. Line up ropes 1 inch apart on a greased baking sheet. Braid loosely, beginning in the middle and working toward ends. (Working from the middle is easier and helps prevent stretching of the dough, which results in an uneven loaf.) Pinch ends of ropes together and tuck the sealed portion under the braid. Cover; let rise in a warm place till almost double (about 40 minutes). Bake in a 325° oven for 30 to 35 minutes or till done. Cover the bread with foil the last 10 to 15 minutes to prevent overbrowning. Cool. Drizzle with Confectioner's Icing. Sprinkle with pecan halves and cherries, if desired. Makes 1 braid.

Confectioner's Icing: In a small mixing bowl stir together 1 cup sifted *powdered sugar*, ¼ teaspoon *vanilla*, and enough *milk* to make the icing of drizzling consistency (about 1½ tablespoons).

Chocolate Waffles

Start your day right with these nutty chocolate waffles—

1 beaten egg
¾ cup milk
¼ cup chocolate-flavored syrup
2 tablespoons cooking oil
1 cup packaged pancake mix
⅓ cup chopped pecans
¼ cup chocolate-flavored syrup
¼ cup maple-flavored syrup
  Butter *or* margarine (optional)

In a small mixing bowl combine the egg, milk, ¼ cup chocolate-flavored syrup, and cooking oil. With a whisk or a rotary beater, beat the chocolate mixture till well combined. Place the pancake mix in a medium mixing bowl. Add the chocolate mixture and beat just till combined.

Pour about *half* of the batter onto the grids of a preheated, lightly greased waffle baker. Sprinkle with *half* of the chopped pecans. Close the waffle baker lid quickly; do not open while the waffle is baking. Remove the baked waffle from the grid with a fork. Repeat with remaining batter and nuts. Stir together ¼ cup chocolate-flavored syrup and maple syrup; serve with the waffles. Serve with butter or margarine, if desired. Makes two 9-inch waffles.

Pictured opposite: Chocolate Pecan Braid

Milk Chocolate Bubble Ring

You can prepare this pull-apart coffee cake in about 25 minutes—

2 packages (10 each)
   refrigerated biscuits
20 milk chocolate kisses
½ cup sugar
½ teaspoon ground cinnamon
¼ cup butter *or* margarine,
   melted

Remove the refrigerated biscuits from their packages; separate into individual biscuits (you should have 20 biscuits total). Using your hands, flatten each biscuit into a 2½- to 3-inch round of dough. Unwrap the milk chocolate kisses. Place a chocolate kiss, point side up, in the center of each round of dough. Bring the edge of the dough up and around the chocolate kiss to form a ball. Pinch the edge of the dough together to seal firmly.

In a small mixing bowl combine the sugar and ground cinnamon; stir till well combined. Dip each ball of dough into the melted butter or margarine, then roll it in the sugar-cinnamon mixture. Arrange the coated balls of dough in a greased 6½-cup oven-proof ring mold. Form two layers, positioning the balls of dough in the second layer between the balls of dough in the first layer. Bake in a 375° oven about 20 minutes or till golden brown. Cool 1 minute on a wire rack. Invert onto a serving plate; remove ring mold. Serve coffee cake warm. Makes 1 ring.

How To Make Milk Chocolate Bubble Ring

Place a milk chocolate kiss, point side up, in the center of each round of biscuit dough. Bring the edge of the dough up and around the chocolate kiss to form a ball. Pinch the edge of the dough together to seal firmly.

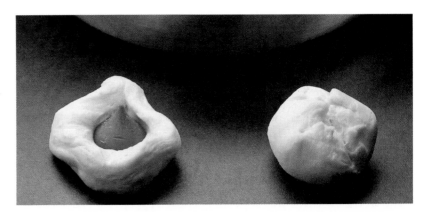

Dip each ball of dough in the melted butter, then roll it in the sugar-cinnamon mixture. Arrange the coated balls of dough in a greased 6½-cup oven-proof ring mold. Form two layers, positioning the balls of dough in the second layer between the balls of dough in the first layer.

Chocolate Banana Nut Bread

What a great way to introduce a new flavor into banana nut bread—

3 squares (3 ounces)
   semisweet chocolate
1½ cups all-purpose flour
1¼ teaspoons baking powder
½ teaspoon baking soda
¼ teaspoon salt
⅔ cup sugar
⅓ cup shortening
2 eggs
1 cup mashed ripe banana
   (about 2 medium bananas)
½ cup chopped nuts

Melt semisweet chocolate (see instructions on page 4); cool. In a small mixing bowl stir together flour, baking powder, baking soda, and salt; set aside.

In a large mixer bowl beat sugar and shortening on medium speed of electric mixer till light, scraping sides of bowl often. Add eggs, one at a time, and the melted chocolate, beating till smooth and fluffy after each addition. Add flour mixture and mashed banana alternately to beaten mixture, beating till smooth after each addition. Fold in nuts. Turn batter into 2 lightly greased 7½x3½x2-inch loaf pans or 1 lightly greased 8x4x2-inch loaf pan. Bake in a 350° oven about 35 minutes for the small loaves or 45 to 50 minutes for the large loaf or till a wooden pick inserted near the center comes out clean. Cool in pans 10 minutes. Remove from pans; cool thoroughly on a wire rack. For easier slicing, wrap loaves in foil and store overnight. Makes 2 small loaves or 1 large loaf.

Cocoa-Raisin Muffins

1¾ cups all-purpose flour
½ cup sugar
3 tablespoons unsweetened
   cocoa powder
2½ teaspoons baking powder
½ teaspoon ground cinnamon
¼ teaspoon salt
⅓ cup chopped nuts
⅓ cup raisins
1 beaten egg
¾ cup milk
⅓ cup cooking oil

In a medium mixing bowl stir together all-purpose flour, sugar, unsweetened cocoa powder, baking powder, cinnamon, and salt; stir in chopped nuts and raisins. Make a well in the center. In a small mixing bowl combine egg, milk, and oil; add all at once to dry ingredients. Stir just till moistened (batter should be lumpy). Grease muffin pan or line with paper bake cups; fill ⅔ full. Bake in a 400° oven for 18 to 20 minutes or till browned. Remove from pans; serve warm. Makes 12 muffins.

Mini-Chip Oatmeal Scones

You can enjoy this English teatime treat on any occasion—

1 cup all-purpose flour
3 tablespoons sugar
2 teaspoons baking powder
⅓ cup butter *or* margarine
1 cup quick-cooking
   rolled oats
½ of a 6-ounce package
   (½ cup) miniature
   semisweet chocolate
   pieces
2 beaten eggs

In a medium mixing bowl stir together flour, sugar, and baking powder. Cut in the butter or margarine till the mixture resembles coarse crumbs. Stir in the oats and miniature semisweet chocolate pieces. Add the beaten eggs and stir till the dry ingredients are moistened (the dough will be sticky). On a lightly floured surface roll or pat the dough into a 7-inch circle. Cut the circle into 12 wedges. Place the wedges on an ungreased baking sheet. Bake in a 400° oven for 10 to 12 minutes or till golden brown. Serve warm. Makes 12 scones.

CHOCOLATE

Beverages

Hot Chocolate

A traditional favorite that can't be beat—

1 cup water
⅓ cup sugar
2 squares (2 ounces) unsweetened chocolate, coarsely chopped
4 cups milk
  Marshmallows *or* whipped cream (optional)

In a medium saucepan combine water, sugar, and unsweetened chocolate. Cook and stir over medium-low heat till chocolate melts. Gradually stir in milk; heat just to boiling. *Do not boil.* Remove the saucepan from the heat; beat mixture with a rotary beater till frothy. Serve hot beverage in coffee cups or mugs. Top each serving with a few marshmallows or a dollop of whipped cream, if desired. Makes 6 (6-ounce) servings.

Coffee Chocolate: Prepare Hot Chocolate as above, *except* stir 2 tablespoons instant *coffee crystals* into chocolate-water mixture before heating.

Spicy Chocolate: Prepare Hot Chocolate as above, *except* stir 1 teaspoon ground *cinnamon* and ¼ teaspoon ground *nutmeg* into the chocolate-water mixture before heating.

Hot Cocoa

⅓ cup sugar
⅓ cup unsweetened cocoa powder
½ cup water
3½ cups milk
½ teaspoon vanilla
  Marshmallows *or* whipped cream (optional)

In a medium saucepan combine sugar and unsweetened cocoa powder. Stir in water. Bring mixture to boiling, stirring constantly. Cook and stir 1 minute more. Stir in milk. Heat just to boiling; *do not boil.* Remove the saucepan from heat; stir in vanilla. Beat mixture with a rotary beater till frothy. Serve hot beverage in coffee cups or mugs. Top each serving with a few marshmallows or whipped cream, if desired. Makes 5 (6-ounce) servings.

Hot Cocoa Mix

1 8-quart package (10 cups) nonfat dry milk powder
1 16-ounce package (about 4¾ cups) sifted powdered sugar
1 16-ounce can (2 cups) presweetened cocoa powder
1 6-ounce jar (1¾ cups) powdered non-dairy creamer
  Marshmallows *or* whipped cream (optional)

To make the hot cocoa mix, in a large mixing bowl combine the nonfat dry milk powder, sifted powdered sugar, presweetened cocoa powder, and non-dairy creamer. Stir till thoroughly combined. Store the hot cocoa mix in airtight containers. Makes about 15 cups mix.

To serve, place ⅓ cup hot cocoa mix in a coffee cup or mug; add ¾ cup *boiling water*. Stir to dissolve cocoa mix. Top with a few marshmallows or whipped cream, if desired. Makes 1 (8-ounce) serving.

Hot Chocolate Malted Mix: Prepare the Hot Cocoa Mix as directed above, *except* use only *half* of a 16-ounce can (1 cup) presweetened cocoa powder and stir 1 cup instant *chocolate malted milk powder* into the dry ingredients.

Mocha Mix: Prepare the Hot Cocoa Mix as directed above, *except* stir one 2-ounce jar (¾ cup) instant *coffee crystals* into the dry ingredients.

*Pictured opposite: Chocolate Crème Liqueur (see recipe, page 89)
Chocolate Cups (see page 91)*

Mexican Chocolate Floats

"Cool it" with these chocolate-cinnamon refreshers—

¼ cup sugar
¼ cup unsweetened cocoa
    powder
½ teaspoon ground cinnamon
2 cups milk
2 cups light cream
1 pint vanilla *or* chocolate
    ice cream (6 scoops)

In a large saucepan combine sugar, cocoa powder, and ground cinnamon. Stir in milk. Cook and stir over low heat till sugar dissolves. Remove from heat. Stir in the light cream. Cover and chill. Before serving, beat the chocolate mixture with a rotary beater till foamy. Place a scoop of vanilla or chocolate ice cream in each of 6 tall glasses; fill with the chocolate mixture. Makes 6 (8-ounce) servings.

Chocolate Milk Shakes

This drink requires little work, but gives lots of pleasure—

1 pint vanilla ice cream
    (2 cups)
1 cup milk
¼ cup chocolate-flavored
    syrup

Place the vanilla ice cream in a blender container. Add the milk and chocolate-flavored syrup to the ice cream. Cover and blend till the chocolate mixture is smooth. Pour the mixture into 2 tall glasses. Serve immediately. Makes 2 (8-ounce) servings.

Choco-Nutty Milk Shakes: Prepare the Chocolate Milk Shakes as directed above, *except* add 2 tablespoons *peanut butter* with the milk.

Mocha Cream Milk Shakes: Prepare the Chocolate Milk Shakes as directed above, *except* stir 2 teaspoons instant *coffee crystals* into the milk.

Choconana Malts

For an additional chocolate boost, use chocolate-flavored milk—

1 cup milk
2 tablespoons instant
    chocolate malted milk
    powder
1 ripe banana, cut up
1 pint chocolate ice cream
    (2 cups)

In a blender container combine the milk and chocolate malted milk powder. Cover and blend till the malted milk powder is dissolved. Add the cut-up banana and chocolate ice cream. Cover and blend till smooth. Pour into 2 tall glasses. Makes 2 (11-ounce) servings.

Chocolate Grasshoppers

Hop to it and indulge in these chocolate-mint delights—

1 pint chocolate ice cream
    (2 cups)
¼ cup white crème de menthe
¼ cup crème de cacao
    Whipped cream (optional)

In a blender container combine chocolate ice cream, crème de menthe, and crème de cacao. Cover and blend just till smooth. Pour into 4 glasses. Dollop each with whipped cream, if desired. Makes 4 (5-ounce) servings.

Mocha Coffee

The marshmallow creme melts quickly and adds richness to this drink—

1   envelope instant cocoa mix
2   teaspoons instant coffee
     crystals
¾ cup boiling water
     Marshmallow creme
     (optional)

In a coffee cup or mug combine the instant cocoa mix and the instant coffee crystals. Stir in boiling water. Dollop with marshmallow creme, if desired. Makes 1 (8-ounce) serving.

Café Israel

2   cups hot strong coffee
½ cup orange liqueur
½ cup chocolate-flavored syrup
     Unsweetened whipped cream
     Finely shredded orange peel
     (optional)

In a 4-cup glass measure or a small mixing bowl combine the hot strong coffee, orange liqueur, and chocolate-flavored syrup. Stir mixture till well combined. Pour into 4 coffee cups or mugs. Dollop each serving with unsweetened whipped cream. Sprinkle with orange peel, if desired. Makes 4 (6-ounce) servings.

Café Colombia: Prepare the Café Israel as directed above, *except* substitute *coffee liqueur* for the orange liqueur and reduce the chocolate-flavored syrup to *¼ cup.*

Chocolate-Orange Sippers

¾ cup orange juice *or* ⅓ cup
     orange liqueur
⅓ cup crème de cacao
     Ice cubes
     Orange slices (optional)

Combine orange juice or orange liqueur and crème de cacao. Pour over ice in 2 glasses. Garnish with orange slices, if desired. Makes 2 (3- or 4½-ounce) servings.

Orange Liqueurs

Liqueurs, often called cordials, come in a delightful variety of fruit flavors. They are not pure distilled spirits because syrup and other flavorings are added to sweeten them. One of these popular liqueurs, used in the Café Israel and the Chocolate-Orange Sippers, is orange liqueur. Among the most widely known orange liqueurs are Grand Marnier, Cointreau, and Curaçao, which are flavored with orange peels. Triple Sec, also widely known, is flavored with cloves and cinnamon, in addition to oranges.

Like other liqueurs, orange liqueurs can be enjoyed plain (straight up), poured over ice (on the rocks), drizzled over scoops of ice cream, or used in beverages and desserts.

Homemade Crème de Cacao

Let the mixture age for 1 week in order to blend the flavors—

2 cups water
1 cup sugar
1 vanilla bean, split
1½ cups vodka
1 tablespoon chocolate extract

In a heavy medium saucepan combine the water, sugar, and vanilla bean. Stir till well combined. Bring the mixture to boiling. Boil gently, uncovered, about 25 minutes or till the liquid is reduced to 1 cup. Remove the saucepan from heat; cool, uncovered, for 30 minutes. Remove the split vanilla bean, if desired. Stir in the vodka and chocolate extract. Transfer to a bottle or jar with a tight-fitting lid. Let the mixture age for 1 week before serving. Store at room temperature. Makes about 2½ cups.

Chocolate Eggnog Deluxe

This thick, rich party drink disappears quickly—

6 egg yolks
¼ cup sugar
2 cups chocolate-flavored milk
½ cup crème de cacao*
½ cup Amaretto*
1 teaspoon vanilla
2 cups whipping cream
6 egg whites
¼ cup sugar
Ground nutmeg

In a small mixer bowl beat the egg yolks on low speed of electric mixer till blended. Gradually add ¼ cup sugar, beating on high speed of electric mixer about 5 minutes or till the egg yolks are thick and lemon colored. Stir in the chocolate-flavored milk, crème de cacao, Amaretto, and vanilla till well combined. Cover and chill thoroughly.

In a large mixer bowl beat the whipping cream on medium speed of electric mixer till soft peaks form. Transfer to another large bowl. Wash beaters and large mixer bowl thoroughly. In the large mixer bowl beat egg whites on medium speed of electric mixer till soft peaks form (tips curl over). Gradually add the remaining ¼ cup sugar, beating on high speed of electric mixer till stiff peaks form (tips stand straight). Fold the egg yolk mixture into the whipped cream; fold in the beaten egg white mixture. Serve immediately. Sprinkle a little nutmeg over each serving. Makes about 22 (4-ounce) servings.

***Note:** For a nonalcoholic eggnog, prepare the Chocolate Eggnog Deluxe as directed above, *except* omit the crème de cacao and the Amaretto and increase the chocolate-flavored milk to *3 cups.*

How To Make Chocolate Eggnog Deluxe

To fold the whipped cream, egg whites, and chocolate mixture together, cut down through mixture with a rubber spatula; scrape across the bottom of bowl and bring the spatula up and over the mixture, as shown in photo.

Chocolate Crème Liqueur

This silky smooth after-dinner drink is pictured on page 84—

1 14-ounce can Eagle Brand
    sweetened condensed milk
1 cup light cream
1 cup milk
2 teaspoons instant coffee
    crystals
1 beaten egg yolk
1 cup Irish whiskey
⅓ cup rum
1 tablespoon chocolate extract
    or 2 tablespoons
    chocolate-flavored syrup
1 tablespoon vanilla

In a heavy large saucepan combine sweetened condensed milk, light cream, milk, and instant coffee crystals. Cook and stir over medium heat till the coffee crystals are dissolved. Gradually stir about *half* of the hot mixture into the beaten egg yolk; return all of the mixture to the saucepan. Bring to a boil. Cook and stir over medium heat for 2 minutes more. Remove the saucepan from heat. Stir in the Irish whiskey, rum, chocolate extract or chocolate-flavored syrup, and vanilla. Cool. Transfer the mixture to a bottle or jar with a tight-fitting lid; chill several hours or overnight. Shake well before serving. If desired, serve in Chocolate Cups (see instructions, page 90). Store, covered, in the refrigerator up to 2 months. Makes about 4½ cups.

Chocolate Crème Custard Sauce: Prepare the Chocolate Crème Liqueur as directed above, *except* use 3 beaten *eggs* instead of 1 beaten egg yolk. Continue as directed, *except* after stirring in the whiskey, rum, chocolate extract or chocolate-flavored syrup, and vanilla, pour the custard mixture into a medium mixing bowl. Cover the surface with clear plastic wrap; chill till serving time. You may spoon the custard sauce over vanilla ice cream, pound cake, or fresh fruit.

Cooking with Carob

If you like the flavor of chocolate, then you might be interested in trying carob. Although carob is similar in appearance to chocolate, it is an entirely different product. Carob, which comes from the pods of the carob tree, contains its own natural sweetness, is low in fat, and is caffeine-free.

You can purchase carob in various forms, the most popular ones being carob chips, carob powder, and candy bars containing carob. Look for these products in supermarkets and health food stores.

When cooking with carob, use the recipes given on the package or ask for recipes when you purchase carob. To adapt your own recipes, try following these guidelines: Use the carob chips to replace *unmelted* semisweet chocolate pieces or milk chocolate pieces. Use powdered carob in the same way you use unsweetened cocoa powder.

To make this change, follow any directions given on the carob package or substitute an equal amount of carob powder for the unsweetened cocoa powder, adjusting the amount of carob to suit your taste, if necessary. Whenever you substitute carob for chocolate or cocoa powder, you may notice some texture and flavor differences. These differences probably will be least noticeable in bar cookies and hot beverages.

Finishing Touches

A garnish of chocolate can make even a simple dessert appear showy. You'll want to try your hand at several garnishes shown here and perhaps create some of your own. To ensure success, make sure the utensils that you use are clean and dry.

Use the type of chocolate that is recommended, and try to handle it as little as possible to keep it from melting. Refrigerate garnishes if you do not use them immediately.

The three finishing touches shown below are basic chocolate garnishes that take little time to make. You can use unsweetened chocolate, semisweet chocolate, or German sweet cooking chocolate for the Grated Chocolate and the Shaved Chocolate. For best results, use milk chocolate for the Chocolate Curls.

Grated Chocolate

Start with a cool, firm square of chocolate and rub it across the grating section of a hand grater. Use the fine grates (top) or the large grates (bottom), depending on the best size for your garnish. Clean the surface of your grater frequently to prevent clogging. Sprinkle chocolate atop cakes, pies, tortes, custards, and frozen desserts.

Shaved Chocolate

For shaved chocolate, you'll need a vegetable peeler and a cool, firm piece of chocolate. Using short, quick strokes, scrape the vegetable peeler across the surface of the chocolate to make irregular shavings. Sprinkle shaved chocolate atop cakes, pies, tortes, custards, and frozen desserts.

Chocolate Curls

Let a bar of chocolate come to room temperature, then carefully draw a vegetable peeler across the chocolate. For small curls, use a narrow side of the chocolate; for large curls, use a wide surface. To transfer a curl without breaking it, insert a wooden pick through one end and lift. Arrange atop tortes, layer cakes, and cheesecakes.

The garnishes below may look elaborate, but they are easy and fun to make. For Chocolate Leaves and Chocolate Cups, use either semisweet or German sweet cooking chocolate. Use a liquid mixture made with cocoa powder and warm water for the Cocoa Painting.

For Chocolate Leaves, select nontoxic fresh leaves, such as mint, lemon, ivy, or strawberry leaves. Wash leaves and pat dry. Melt chocolate (see instructions on page 4) and apply as directed below. You'll need about 3 ounces melted chocolate to coat 6 small fresh leaves.

For Chocolate Cups, use small paper containers, such as candy cups or petit fours cups. (Don't use paper bake cups designed for cupcakes; they are too large to hold their shape after chocolate is applied.) Look for these in supermarkets or stores that sell candy-making supplies.

Chocolate Leaves

With a small paintbrush, brush melted chocolate on the underside of each fresh leaf, building up layers of chocolate so garnish will be sturdy. Wipe off chocolate that may have run onto front of leaf. Place on a waxed-paper-lined baking sheet; chill or freeze till hardened. Just before using, peel fresh leaf away from the chocolate leaf, as shown in the photo.

Chocolate Cups

Melt chocolate. With a small paintbrush, brush melted chocolate onto bottom and up side of each paper candy cup till about ⅛ inch thick, as shown in the photo. Wipe off any chocolate that may have run over the top. Chill or freeze till hardened. To serve, peel paper cup away from chocolate cup. Fill cups with liqueur, cream for coffee, or small candy and nuts.

Cocoa Painting

Combine 1 tablespoon unsweetened *cocoa powder* and 1 tablespoon warm *water.* With a small paintbrush, paint a design atop cookies or cakes using the cocoa mixture. Decorate cookies or cakes that have a thoroughly dried light-colored frosting. If cocoa mixture becomes thick, stir in more warm water. Let design dry for 15 to 20 minutes.

These impressive garnishes use a decorating bag and writing tip. Simply melt together 2 squares (2 ounces) *semisweet chocolate* and 1 teaspoon *butter or margarine* (see instructions on page 4). Cool about 20 minutes.

For the Chocolate Butterflies, cut a sheet of waxed paper into 3x2-inch rectangles. Fold each in half crosswise, forming a 2x1½-inch rectangle. Using a pencil, draw an outline of half of a butterfly, including the body and antenna. Press down hard with the pencil to form outline on bottom half of the waxed paper. Open the waxed paper and place it on a flat work surface; tape to surface. Pipe the chocolate mixture and shape each butterfly as directed below.

For the Chocolate Piping, pipe the chocolate in a free-form design or in a written message as directed below.

Chocolate Butterflies

Fit a decorating bag with a small writing tip. Spoon the cooled chocolate mixture into the bag. Pipe the chocolate mixture in a steady line onto each piece of waxed paper, following the butterfly outline. Pipe additional lines to fill in the wings. Let stand about 20 minutes or till the chocolate begins to set up.

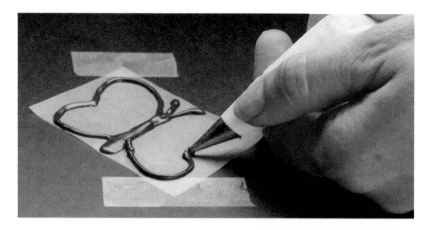

After the chocolate begins to set up, remove tape from waxed paper. Carefully slide a wide spatula under each piece of waxed paper; transfer to an inverted egg carton, placing butterfly between the cups so it is slightly bent at the center fold. (The wings should be in a semi-open position.) Chill about 30 minutes or till chocolate hardens. Carefully peel waxed paper away from the chocolate butterflies.

Chocolate Piping

Spoon cooled chocolate mixture into a decorating bag fitted with a writing tip. Pipe the chocolate mixture in steady lines to create a design or write a message. You can pipe the chocolate directly onto a cake or cookie and chill till hardened. Or, you can pipe designs onto waxed paper, chill till hardened, and then transfer to the dessert.

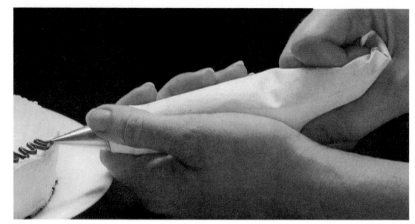

The Candy Bar Border is an easy garnish that appeals to kids. When you use it to ring a cake, make sure frosting is moist so candy sections will adhere to the side. But don't limit this idea to cakes. Line edges of dessert dishes with candy sections before filling with ice cream or pudding.

Chocolate Cutouts and Chocolate Ribbons add special touches to many desserts. Arrange cutouts atop cakes and pies or let them peek out from a mound of whipped cream. If you make more than you can use at one time, cover and refrigerate the extras. The

ribbons add a dramatic look to desserts when draped atop individual servings. They also work well for lining glass dessert dishes before filling with creamy desserts. Just let the ribbons stand at room temperature about 15 minutes to give them the flexibility to bend easily.

Candy Bar Border

For a quick and clever cake garnish, create a candy bar border. For an 8x1½-inch round cake, use four 1.45-ounce bars *milk chocolate;* divide each bar into 12 sections. Arrange the candy bar sections, smooth side out, around the freshly frosted cake, as shown in the photo. Chill till serving time. Cut cake between the candy bar sections to serve.

Chocolate Cutouts

Melt together one 6-ounce package *semisweet chocolate pieces* and 1 tablespoon *butter or margarine* (see instructions on page 4); cool. Pour onto a waxed-paper-lined baking sheet, spreading ¼ to ⅛ inch thick. Chill till almost set. Firmly press hors d'oeuvre or cookie cutters into chocolate. Chill. Before serving, lift cutouts from baking sheet.

Chocolate Ribbons

Prepare chocolate mixture as directed for Chocolate Cutouts; cool. Pour onto waxed-paper-lined baking sheet. Top with a second sheet of waxed paper. Roll chocolate to ⅛-inch thickness. Chill till firm. Peel off top layer of waxed paper. Let stand at room temperature for 15 minutes. Using a fluted pastry wheel or knife, cut chocolate into strips, as shown in photo.

Index